Raymond Rush

The Last Man Standing

Raymond Rush
The Last Man Standing

The Last of The Expendables
1st Battalion, The South Lancs Regiment

Written by John Kelly

Dedicated to all those men who didn't return.

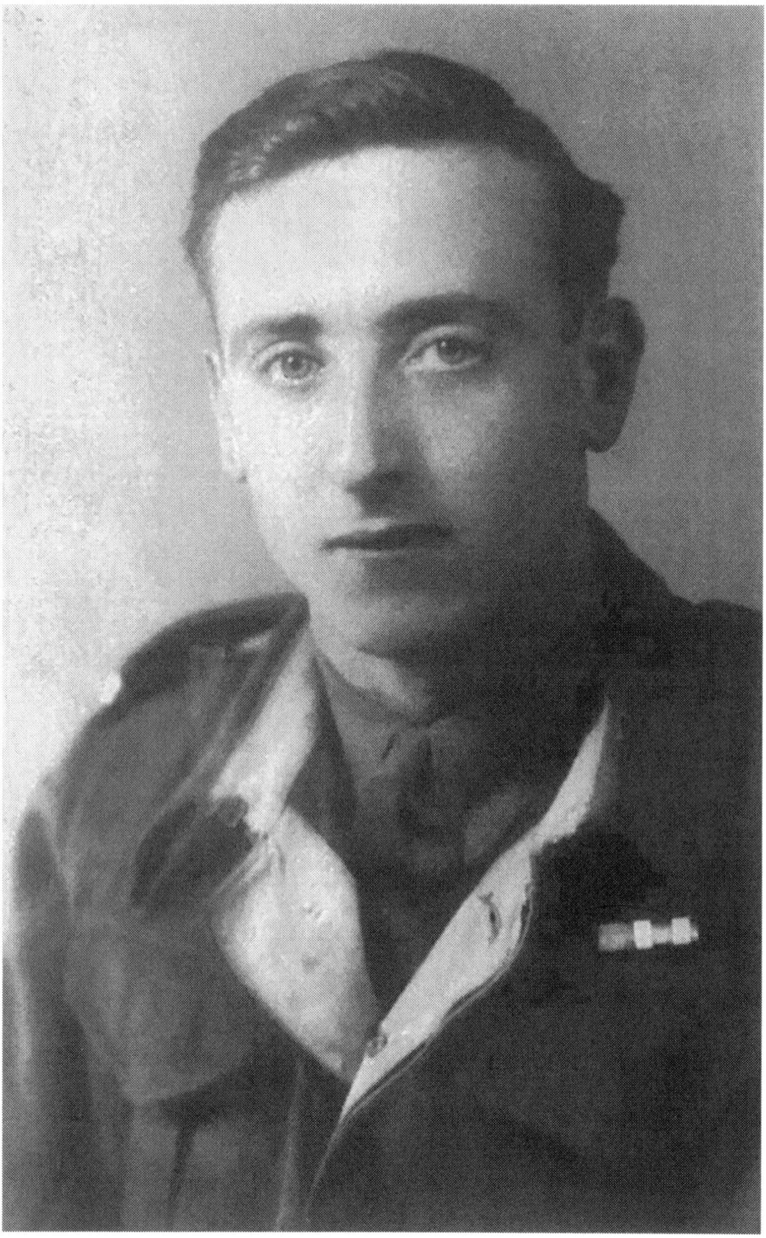

Foreword

I met Raymond through the local Armed Forces and Veterans breakfast club, where veterans from all services would meet once a week to eat breakfast or drink tea and coffee and catch up with each other on news and current events. Just like the old days, some of the banter and leg-pulling would seem controversial to the non-military person but, for those used to it, it was a way to "get back to the tribe," so to speak.

Raymond would sit quietly and mainly keep himself to himself. He would watch and smile at the jokes. There was a serenity about him and, of course, because of who he is, most held him in awe and left him alone. We affectionately called him "The Colonel". But if you sat and talked to him you very soon saw he had a quick and sharp mind. Constantly smiling. He was a joy to be with. When he got to know you better, he would quietly tell you some of his stories from the war and of his life as a boy and young man. He could remember the most intimate detail. He was 96-years-old on December 20th 2019 but his memories were crystal clear. He remembered people and places. He remembered dates and events. It quickly became evident to us all that Raymond was a very special person and his arrival at breakfast club was eagerly anticipated. We became friends. When he asked me to help with his story I was delighted to be involved.

In this book he speaks honestly and frankly about his life in the Second World War. He gives us a remarkable glimpse into his work on the Front Line and in the societies in which he lived before the war and afterwards. The opinions he expresses are his own opinions and they sometimes differ from my own, but this is Raymond Rush's story. He wanted to call this book *The Last Man Standing*, the reason being is that, at the end of the war, he was the sole surviving member of his original Company of Brothers. All the rest who had landed with him on D-Day in those first waves were dead, wounded or captured. What is even more remarkable is that, on researching Ray's story, I came into contact with and received the support of the staff of the Fulwood barracks museum of the Lancashire Infantry Regiments, who told me that they thought none of the 1st South Lancs were still with us. They did not know about Raymond. The histories of the war had been written mostly by the officers and by journalists who followed afterwards, when the work of Raymond Rush and The Expendables to clear the way for them had already begun. Afterwards, only one man was still standing.

John Kelly, 2020

SUPREME HEADQUARTERS
ALLIED EXPEDITIONARY FORCE

Soldiers, Sailors and Airmen of the Allied Expeditionary Force!

You are about to embark upon the Great Crusade, toward which we have striven these many months. The eyes of the world are upon you. The hopes and prayers of liberty-loving people everywhere march with you. In company with our brave Allies and brothers-in-arms on other Fronts, you will bring about the destruction of the German war machine, the elimination of Nazi tyranny over the oppressed peoples of Europe, and security for ourselves in a free world.

Your task will not be an easy one. Your enemy is well trained, well equipped and battle-hardened. He will fight savagely.

But this is the year 1944! Much has happened since the Nazi triumphs of 1940-41. The United Nations have inflicted upon the Germans great defeats, in open battle, man-to-man. Our air offensive has seriously reduced their strength in the air and their capacity to wage war on the ground. Our Home Fronts have given us an overwhelming superiority in weapons and munitions of war, and placed at our disposal great reserves of trained fighting men. The tide has turned! The free men of the world are marching together to Victory!

I have full confidence in your courage, devotion to duty and skill in battle. We will accept nothing less than full Victory!

Good Luck! And let us all beseech the blessing of Almighty God upon this great and noble undertaking.

Dwight D. Eisenhower

Reproduced courtesy of the Robert Pearson Collection, 2019

Preface

Field Marshal Erwin Rommel, the German hero of the Afrika Corps in North Africa, had built his wall well. The Atlantic Wall stretched from Norway to the France-Spain border and was the Germans' defence against an Allied invasion of Western Europe. The designated British D-Day beaches alone had a string of German strongpoints called Wiedestandnest (Nest of resistance), eighty-seven of them strung out along the coast to directly oppose any attempt by the Allied forces to land. Sword beach, where Raymond Rush and the South Lancs would land, on the morning of the 6th of June, had twenty of these formidable strongpoints, each with one or two 88mm guns, several machine-guns, a large number of mortar pits and massed infantry support. In between and in front of these strongpoints were tank traps, fields of barbed wire and high density minefields.

The Russians, fighting for their lives in the east, were constantly pressing the Allies to mount a second front in the west to relieve some of the pressure on their forces. In June 1944, the Allies were ready. The Second Front was about to begin. 24,000 Paratroopers and airborne forces and 132,000 seaborne forces were about to invade Normandy. The South Lancs were ready to spearhead the British seaborne attack to liberate Europe from Nazi tyranny.

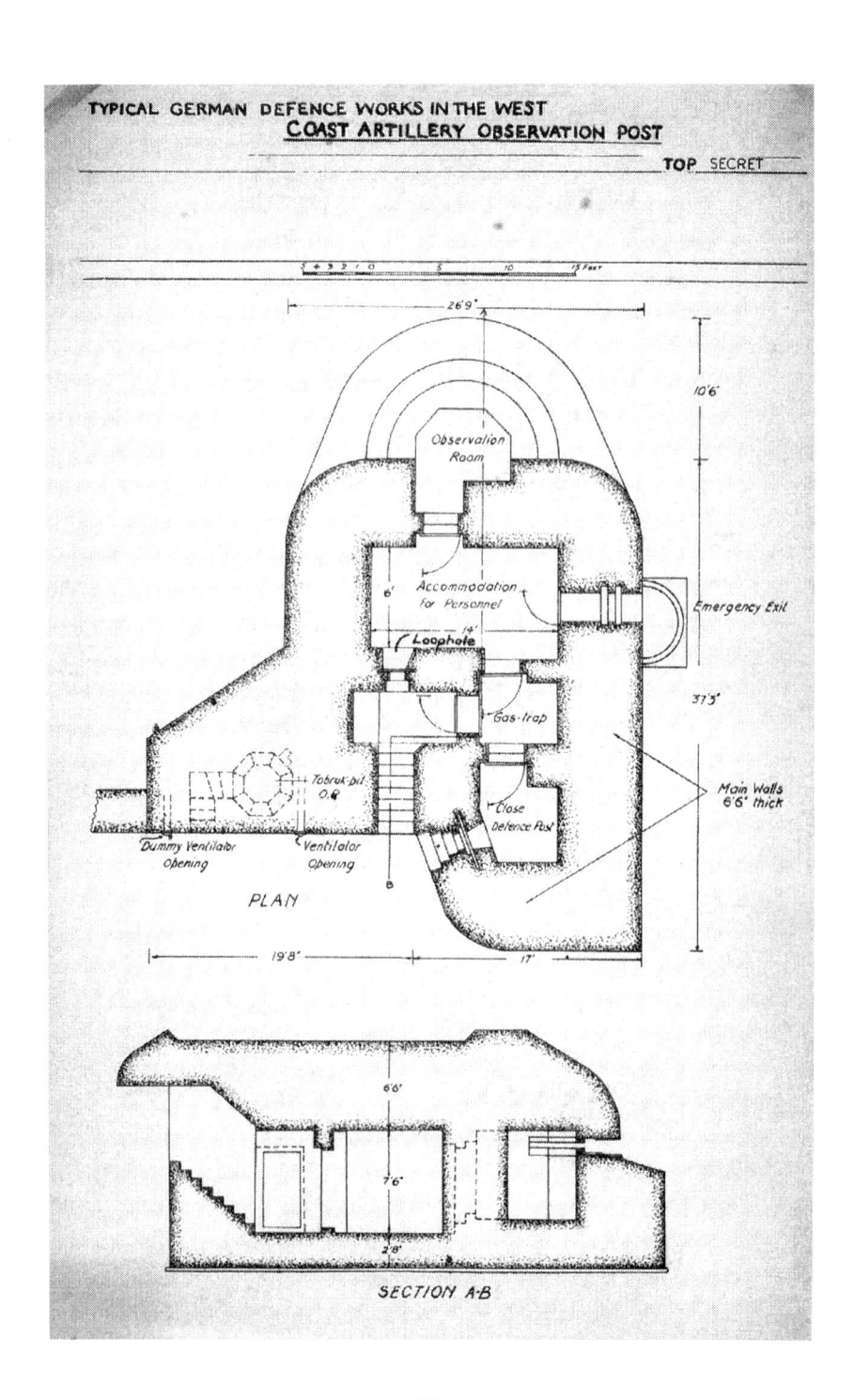

TYPICAL GERMAN DEFENCE WORKS IN THE WEST
COAST ARTILLERY OBSERVATION POST

TOP SECRET

TYPICAL GERMAN DEFENCE WORKS IN THE WEST

TOP SECRET

PILLBOX WITH 75mm A/TK GUN -

Scale 1:200

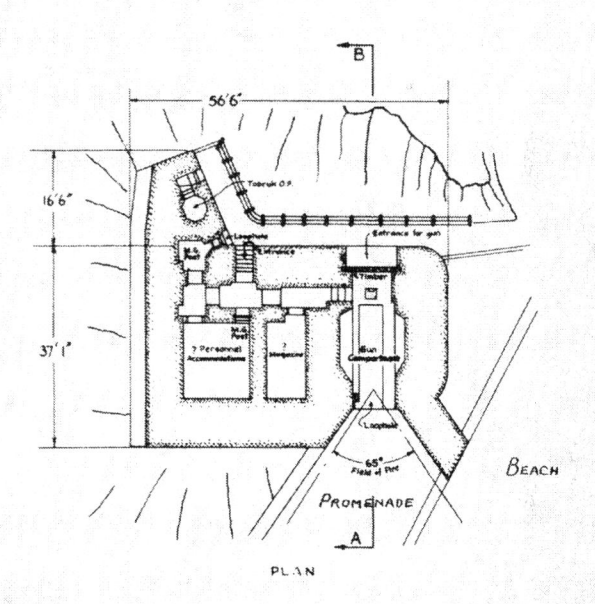

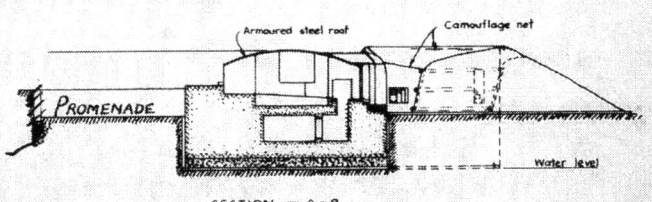

PLAN

SECTION — A-B

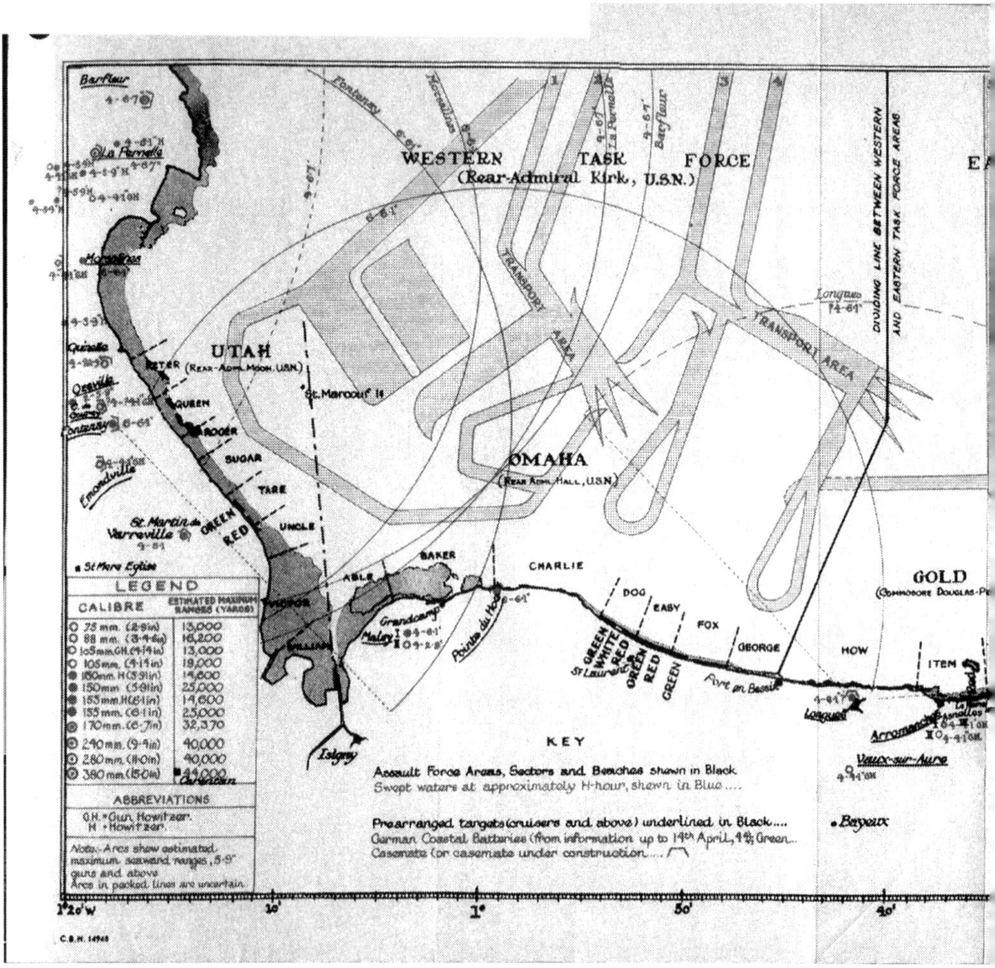
WESTERN TASK FORCE
(Rear-Admiral Kirk, U.S.N.)
UTAH
(Rear-Adml. Moon, U.S.N.)
OMAHA
(Rear Adml. Hall, U.S.N.)
GOLD
TRANSPORT AREA
TRANSPORT AREA
DIVIDING LINE BETWEEN WESTERN AND EASTERN TASK FORCE AREAS
Barfleur
La Pernelle
Quineville
Fontenay
Emondeville
St. Martin de Varreville
St Mere Eglise
St. Marcouf Is
PETER
QUEEN
ROGER
SUGAR
TARE
UNCLE
VICTOR
WILLIAM
GREEN
RED
ABLE
BAKER
CHARLIE
DOG
EASY
FOX
GEORGE
HOW
ITEM
Grandcamp
Maisy
Pointe du Hoe
St Laurent
Port en Bessin
Longues
Arromanches
Vaux-sur-Aure
Bayeux
Isigny
Carentan
LEGEND
CALIBRE
ESTIMATED MAXIMUM RANGES (YARDS)
75 mm. (2·9in) 13,000
88 mm. (3·4·6in) 16,200
105mm.G.H.(4·14in) 13,000
105mm. (4·14in) 19,000
150mm. H.(5·91in) 14,600
150mm. (5·91in) 25,000
155mm.H.(6·1in) 14,600
155mm. (6·1in) 25,000
170mm. (6·7in) 32,370
240mm. (9·4in) 40,000
280mm. (11·0in) 40,000
380mm. (15·0in) 44,000
ABBREVIATIONS
G.H. = Gun Howitzer.
H = Howitzer.
Note.- Arcs show estimated maximum seaward ranges, 5·9" guns and above
Arcs in pecked lines are uncertain.
KEY
Assault Force Areas, Sectors and Beaches shown in Black
Swept waters at approximately H-hour, shown in Blue....
Prearranged targets (cruisers and above) underlined in Black....
German Coastal Batteries (from information up to 14th April, 44) Green...
Casemate (or casemate under construction.....
1°20'W
10'
1°
50'
40'
C.B.H. 14948

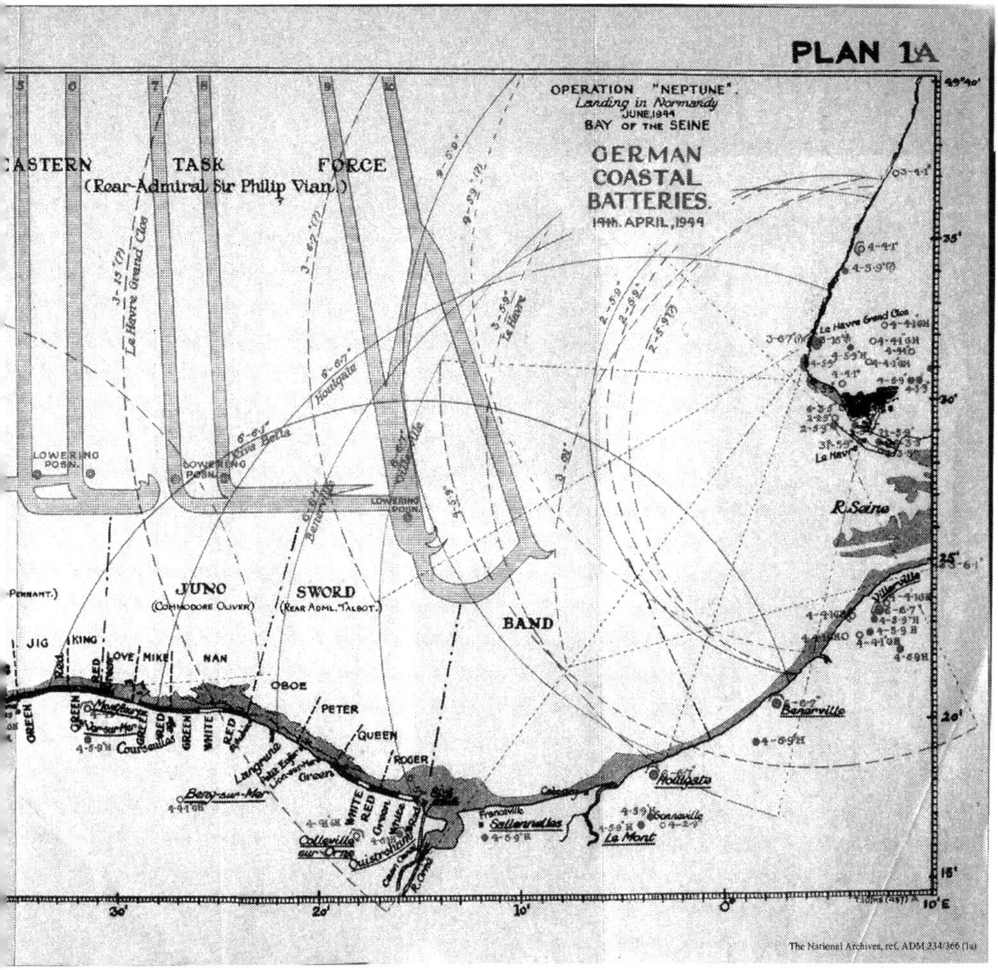

The National Archives, ref. ADM 234/366 (1a)

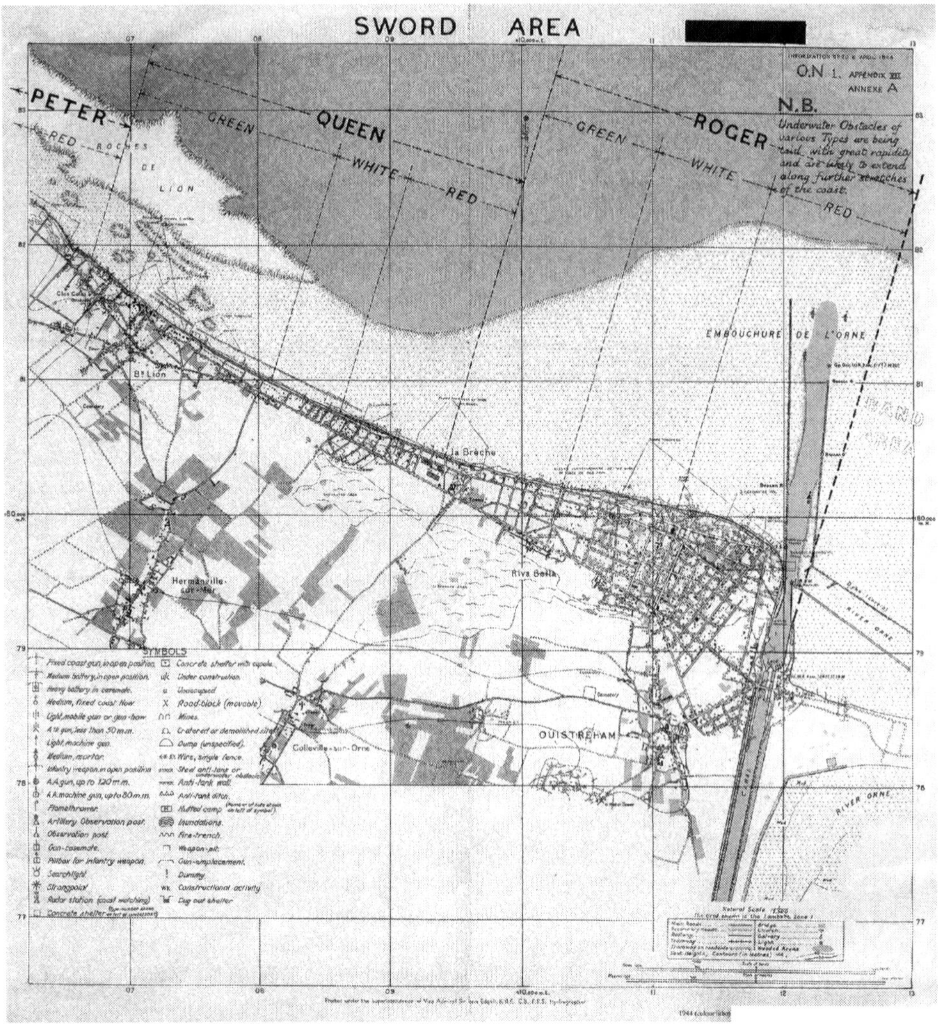

Chapter One

D-Day 6 JUNE 1944
SWORD BEACH

The British 3rd Infantry Division, 8th Assault Brigade, were designated to be Task Force S (for Sword). Raymond Rush and the 1st Battalion South Lancs were the spearhead. They were destined for Sword beach, sectors Queen Red and Queen White. Raymond and the 1st Battalion would land on Queen White on the right flank, facing the village of Colleville-sur-Mer. They would be the first British troops to punch a hole in Hitler's Atlantic wall and the first to push through to liberate France and Europe.

The beginning of 1944 saw the 1st Battalion in Scotland. It was an open secret that the 8th Infantry Brigade would be involved in the Second Front and the 1st Battalion South Lancs would have a prominent part to play in the first phase of the assault landings. They were engaged in intensive assault training and carried out several amphibious training exercises. In early March, they were stationed between Aviemore and Grantown in the far wild north of Scotland. It is an unforgiving land of high snowcapped mountains and long wet river valleys. It is difficult to survive and live in this harsh world, but it would prove to be the best training area for young soldiers soon to be taking on the Nazi fanatics in France. The lofty Cairngorm Mountains were within easy reach for strenuous and intense physical training and large numbers of reinforcements joined them there.

Raymond Rush: I was based at Formby [1] for my basic training. We became skilled in all the weapons available to us, but we never learned how to fight in built-up areas, we did a lot of marching and running up and down sand dunes. Over three days we'd march twenty to thirty miles per day with all our kit on. We'd billet over night where ever there was enough space for the regiment. We could stay anywhere, a farmer's field or anywhere. Nowhere was out of bounds to us.

---
1. Sandy beach in north-west England, popular with daytrippers from Liverpool.

I had a mouth organ. The Sergeant-Major would say, "Play us a tune, Rushy Lad." I'd play all the tunes that I knew from memory to keep up morale. At some point I would be playing and trying to catch my breath at the same time from the marching.

On the rare occasions I got leave, I travelled home to Prescot. I often met up with my cousin Irene, who lived in Thatto Heath (St. Helens) and we'd go to the movies. I always ensured she got home okay before I walked the four miles back to my own home. It was the Black Out. It was pitch black. No matter where you turned there were no lights whatsoever. You had to navigate your own way in the pitch black.

We were walking down the road in Prescot one time and I had my uniform on. Now my cousin Irene was a cracking piece and, as were walking, I thought, "Bloody hell there's a gang of blokes in our way."

I could see this gang a bit further down the road.

"Never mind 'em," Irene says. "They're only bloody Yanks."

She strode right through them, so I thought I'd follow her. They weren't allowed to touch a couple or bother a woman out with a bloke. One of them tripped me though, and I was pissed off. I thought, "There's going to be trouble now." I went down on the floor. I got up and we were nose to nose. "Don't touch me," I shouted at him.

I don't remember what happened next but I ended up with a black eye. I don't know if he did. I get home and I walk into the house and everybody starts arguing, me, dad and my uncle Tommy. It turned into a scrap.

The Yanks had a Dance Hall at Burtonwood but I wouldn't be seen dead there. I didn't rate them as soldiers. They were just over here flashing their money and chasing the women.

On another occasion, on the long walk home, I heard a voice in the dark asking if I needed any help. I thought it was a bit weird. I replied with "What?" He asked me if I needed any help with washing or sewing? If I needed anything fixing? I replied that I had big holes in my socks, from the constant marching. He said, "Follow me then." So I did, cautiously. I was led to a church hall, where by candle-light they darned my socks for me. The locals would do anything to help the war effort.

After initial infantry training, Raymond and his best friend, John Mather, were sent to a training camp in Hereford to what would become the UK base for the SAS (Special Air Service Regiment). There he would be trained up in physical exercise whilst enjoying hearty rations of food to help build him up. Raymond wasn't very big and it was decided that this extra training would get him ready him for the actions to come. The battalion had become a highly trained and integrated infantry unit, tremendously fit physically. Morale was high.

Raymond Rush: I got a weekend pass, most of which was taken up hitchhiking home. There were hardly any cars or vehicles on the road, but no one would refuse you a lift if you were in uniform. I got to Liverpool and I went to see the wrestling. I loved watching wrestling. I recognised one of the wrestlers from my training in Hereford. He was one of the Sergeant instructors who were training us. He was a big stocky bloke. Very firm but fair. We later became friends. On parade on the Monday morning, he came up to me and asked where had I been? I knew he had recognised me at the wrestling, he'd seen my uniform, and he knew full well where I'd been. I told him, "I was at the wrestling and so was he." He told me to keep stum. He was moonlighting as a professional wrestler.

He wrestled under a stage name and was quite a decent wrestler. When he left to go on active service he handed me a shoulder flash, which said 'Second SAS regiment'. It was then that I realised I was being trained by the SAS. At one time, a rumour was spread that we were going to join the Chindit [2] at Burma. We expected to be issued with jungle gear. But we didn't. We were given the most recent assault gear which put those rumours to bed. It meant only one thing, we were joining the attack to liberate Europe.

On 18th March 1944, one of our commanders, General Sir Douglas Baird visited to address the men and officers. After three further days of assault landing exercises, Raymond and the South Lancs moved to Cowplain just North of Portsmouth. Route marches and regular PT kept the men fit and they were trained in house-to-house fighting. On 20th May, a visit by the King at Waterlooville raised morale even further. They were ready. On 25th May, the transit camps were sealed and only under exceptional circumstances would anyone be allowed in or out. Secrecy was of the utmost importance at this stage.

Raymond Rush: We were billeted near Cowplain before we marched down to Portsmouth and got on the ships. We were in tents, twenty men per tent, like big marquees they were. While we were there, we got new recruits, so the whole battalion was in one place and up to full strength. Barbed wire all over the place. The military police would arrest anyone caught outside the wire without a valid excuse. But people took their chances and got under the wire to have a cheeky pint of stout at a local pub. We got a visitor, the Divisional Commander, General Richie [3]. He wanted to talk to the troops. He gave us a pep talk about what we were doing and that picked everyone up. We were mixed up with all sorts. There were Yanks everywhere. Cards game were rife, hustlers earned themselves small fortunes but I lost all my money playing cards because I was never any good at it, three card brag it was. We did drill and polished

---

2. The largest group of Allied special forces.
3. Commanding General of XII Corps.

our kit. We knew that the Germans were very organized in what they did, they always followed orders. We were excited and there was anticipation about what we were going to be doing. We all wished we were off to the desert joining the 7th army, the Desert Rats. I always wanted one of them rat's badges on my shoulder.

The Ox and Bucks (Oxford and Buckinghamshire Light Infantry) were there. They had already seen action and thought they were the bee's knees, strutting about the place.

To break the boredom, there was troop entertainment in one of the big tents. Singer Joan Piper came to sing for us. Tommy Trinder came as well. He was a cockney comedian, bloody rubbish him. He got booed off. You know Vera Lynn was one of the boys. She was really genuine and she loved everybody. You could put your arm round her and she didn't mind. Her husband was always with her. He was a member of her orchestra. She used to go and sing for the troops in all the worst war zones and there was a bloke who went with her wherever she went and he played the piano for her. I used to imagine him lugging that piano about to all these war zones while she sang. She's still singing now I think and she's over a hundred!

I carried a picture of the Queen in my pocket all through the war because I didn't really have a girlfriend then. My mum sent me magazines and I got the picture out of one of them. She used to write and tell me what was going on. We got stuff for the troops, parcels, and we were told to pick what we wanted. So me and Peter Kearney from Widnes got stuck in, we took all sorts.

I bumped into Peter after the war. I was walking down the road and I saw this bloke hobbling towards me. I recognised his outline. It was Pete. He'd lost his leg from the hip downwards in the Battle of the Ardennes Forest. That's when the Brits had to step in when the Germans broke the American line at the Battle of the Bulge. Pete had a wooden leg, solid wood from hip to toe, but he'd learned how to walk with it.

Down in Portsmouth before D-Day there were Brits, Yanks, Poles, all sorts together and there were fights all over the place, shouting at each other, "We should go in first! No it should be us!" Me and my mate, John Mather, started scrapping and ended up on the floor again. The Yanks buggered off and just left two of 'em with us. There was fighting all the time then. The MPs were soon on the scene. They were never far away and seemed to come from nowhere. The Yank MPs had white caps and ours were red. One wrong thing said about your battalion and it could all kick off again. A cry of "Fight!" and the pubs would empty. Everybody piled in.

   Morale was high on the eve of D-Day but one man wouldn't stop crying. He never shut up. There was lots of squaddie banter and fooling about and the Scousers were always telling jokes and making everyone laugh. We were only there for a few days. A few blokes sneaked off, they had enough of it. We didn't know they were going, they just went. I presume they went AWOL. I never saw them again.

Hitler and his intelligence service were convinced the invasion would come from the South East coast of Kent, Dover to Calais. The deceptions were still working. On 26th May, the 1st South Lancs were given maps, models and photographs to study. The next few days were eaten up with briefings and countless equipment checks. The Brigade assembled in Portsmouth before boarding the ships on the 3rd of June that would launch their landing craft.

Raymond Rush: We were told. "Pack your kit and get fell in in battalion order." We were lined up in battalions and quick-marched down to Portsmouth, then we stopped. Thousands of men were all going the same way. We were marched out of the camp from our billets and through the gate,. We marched through the night. It was early morning and I saw it looked all foggy above everybody's heads, but it wasn't fog, it was sweat rising off the soldiers. Then we were marched onto a boat and ordered to stop.

   "Right," we were told. "Steady as you go".
   "We're on the Daffodil here", somebody said.
   "I'm not going on that again."

The MV Daffodil was the practice ship we had trained on.

"Where the bloody hell are we?" I said to another South Lancs man. There were thousands of men on these ships. I then we realized we were not going to the 8th Army or to the desert. We were packed so tight nobody could sit or lie down, I could only stand up and we were all leaning on each other. "Pack em in, pack em in," we were told. And more and more men were pushed on.

A grey unsettled dawn on the 4th June saw the Force S invasion fleet raise their anchors, slip their moorings and slowly edge out of Portsmouth harbor. All along the southern English coast, the assault ships were easing themselves from their moorings and turning for France. The greatest armada the world had ever known was at last on its way. On the shoulders of young men like Raymond rested the hopes of the free world. Failure was too bitter to contemplate.

Raymond Rush: "Right lads," the Sergeant Major said, "at ease, relax and get your heads down if you can."

I could feel the boat rocking and my feet weren't touching the floor.

"Are we moving?"

"Of course we're bloody moving!" Our officers were with us so give them their due there. Our C.O. Major Johnson was a cracking bloke, and I was with him at the Château, but he got killed later on. We still didn't know where we were going. We knew the Allies had landed in Sicily, so we thought maybe we're going there. I thought, "any road, we're in action now," so I put one up the spout and got myself ready.

For the first time Raymond and the South Lancs were told their destination and what were their objectives. They were to go ashore at Luc-sur-Mer near Ouistrahem. Britain had been fighting alone for almost five years. She was a country beset by war, the threat of invasion, bombings and the daily destruction of their homes. Civilian casualties were mounting and her people went to sleep praying for an end. Unknown to anyone, and as the people slept, the great crusade had begun that would rid the world of Nazi tyranny. The transport ships fired up their boilers, set their course for the Normandy beaches and departed for France. To a mixture of disappointment and frustration the weather turned terrible and the ships were recalled after just a few hours.

D-Day hung in the balance. It was being dictated to by the unpredictable English Channel weather. The men in the assault ships had to wait a further 24 hours for the decision to go. Some of the men, those who had the furthest to go, had been on the ships for five days so, to them, a small additional delay was bearable. Every man wanted to get going however and they eagerly awaited the change in the weather and the orders to set sail once more. A brief acceptable, although marginal, window of settled weather was forecast for the 6th, which was all that was needed. The order was sent out again and once more the invasion ships set sail. The ships picked up speed pushing high bow waves and leaving moonlit bathed silver streams of wake behind them.

Just past midnight on the 5th, airborne troops and paratroopers began to land behind the Normandy coast. They quickly completed their tasks and seized their objectives and began to fight to consolidate until the seaborne troops would arrive a few hours later to support and relieve.

At 0300hrs, a massive aerial and naval bombardment of the coastal defenses and artillery emplacements on and behind Sword Beach began.

Reproduced courtesy of Robert Pearson Collection, 2019

Swarms of British and American bombers blitzed the German positions and the beaches. Off the British invasion beaches, HMS Orion, HMS Ajax, HMS Argonaut and HMS Emerald swung to broadside, dropped their anchors and opened fire. The German defenders, battle hardened troops of the 716 Infantry Division, must have been terrified. Twenty-nine Companies, manning over 500 machine-guns, 50 mortars and 90 other calibre guns, cowered in their concrete and steel bunkers, watched and waited, hoping the bombardment would soon stop.

Raymond Rush: The ships' guns started firing and somebody said, "Is that shooting at us?"

"Are they bugger," I said. "It's the ships' guns behind us shooting. They're softening the beaches up."

We were going for so long I could tell the water was deeper because of the way the ship was splashing and the way the waves were. I was 19-years-old and I was getting shit scared now. "Hey Rushy," somebody said. "Where do you think we're going? I'm coming with you."

I could hear the guns from the battleships all around us and firing behind us but we couldn't understand who they were firing at. We could tell after a bit what the sound of our guns were and the different sound of the German guns shooting back. You never forget something like that. It only took a few minutes. Somebody said jokingly, "It's Formby beach. Where's that Sergeant Major? Get him in front of us!"

At 0430hrs, those men of the South Lancs who had been able to snatch a few winks of sleep were woken up and made ready. It was a black night and the cold sea wind chilled already frightened young men. The assault ships sped on through the night with their screws at maximum revolutions. There were so many ships in this armada that they covered the sea and they were all heading for the same place.

D-Day dawned a dull grey morning with the sea still running rough. The men could see an ominous red glow on the southern horizon, the result of the overnight and early morning bombing raids by the RAF and the USAF. The sun rose at 0558hrs into a grey cloud-filled sky.

There was a high swell. Spray flicked off the crests of the waves and white horses raced across the surface of the choppy, wind-blown sea. The men in the assault ships, unused to life at sea, were tossed around mercilessly and more than one had stomach ache from constant retching. The pitching and rolling decks were awash with the bitter contents of men's stomachs. The wind, although light at three to four knots, felt cold and there was a bitter bite that chilled the sweat running down men's backs. Two hours before the men were scheduled to land, the naval bombardment stopped with a final blast and belch of white smoke from the warships guns. The last shells sped towards the enemy. Sailors aboard breathed easier for the first time in hours, their work done for now they could only watch as the assault ships sped past their anchor points and said silent prayers as they handed the fight over to the infantry.

Raymond Rush: All of a sudden silence fell, only a few 25 pounders were still firing. The ship went slower. We had had no food or drink, just water. I could have done with a brew up. The water got deeper and deeper. You could tell by the sound of the water against the ship's side, and we saw fish jumping all over. That quietened a few of the men down. I got no sleep on the ship. I'd had no sleep for weeks.

When we left the ship to get on the landing craft, we had to climb down a netting over the ship's side. It was very wet and slippery. There was a big swell and if you fell between the ship and the boat you were done for. You'd either be crushed by the boat or left to drown. There was no stopping for you. I slid down most of the net. It was tricky with all the kit we were carrying. "Come on soldier," said a voice to me. "We'll look after you." He was a Canadian driving the torpedo boat we were in. He stood above us on a tower driving and he said, "Don't worry about it."

I said, "Are you sure you're alright up there."

"Don't worry about me," he said. "Take your time, take it easy and don't rush." He gave the impression of a guy who knew what to do. We were all apprehensive but he commanded calmness throughout the boat.

Engineers, whose tasks it was to clear beach defences and access points, to allow movement on and off the beach, loaded into their landing craft first and, with belches of diesel exhaust, they left the safety of the assault ships and headed through the swell towards the beach. They had twenty minutes to clear the beach before "H" hour and the first of the South Lancs' attack. Right behind them were the landing craft that would launch the swimming tanks that the South Lancs would need as support during their assault.

0615hrs and the landing craft, loaded with the men of the South Lancs, were seven kilometres offshore and heading as fast as they could race towards the beaches. Concentrating on sectors Queen Red and Queen White, they headed for the village of Hermanville-sur-Mer.

0652hrs and the German 352nd Artillery Regiment reported sixty to eighty landing craft approaching their positions near the eastern section of Colleville-sur-Mer. The Germans waited. They had infested the coastline with wooden stakes, mines, steel hedgehog anti-tank obstacles and reinforced concrete dragons teeth obstacles. They hoped to God that that would be enough to stop any Allied invasion and push them back into the sea. German infantry manned a vast network of trenches, machine-gun nests and mortar pits. Barbed wire surrounded these positions and lined the beach. The beach front itself, being generally flat and exposed, was guarded by bunkers; with machine-gun and sniper posts located in some of the holiday homes and houses lining the shore.

To reinforce the defences, six strongpoints had been constructed, each with at least eight 5cm Pak thirty-eight 50mm anti-tank guns, four 75mm guns, and one 88mm gun. One of the strongpoints, codenamed COD, faced directly onto Queen beach. Exits from the beaches had been blocked with various obstacles and vast rivers of barbed wire. Behind the beaches, six artillery batteries had been positioned, three of which were based within three strong-points.

These latter batteries had four 100 mm guns and up to ten 155mm guns and all were ranged for Sword beach.

0720hrs and 19-year-old Raymond Rush and the South Lancs are five minutes from the beach. The landings across the Normandy beaches were following the tide eastwards, so Sword beach was the last. The weather was marginal and there was a strong off-shore riptide. Usually a beach would be assaulted by the infantry formed into three battalions abreast but, because of a shoal of off-shore rocks, the 1st South Lancs were forced to assault with only two battalions on a much reduced frontage. The two battalions, Raymond amongst them, would be in the first wave. Their divisional comrades, the East Yorks were further to their left, assaulting the sector next to them. The South Lancs had been warned that the defences would be extensive and the beach would be heavily defended. In each of the South Lancs battalions were four companies, two in the assault, one in the follow-up, and one in reserve. They were grimly told that they could expect up to 100% casualties in the first wave but they must not stop for anything and must clear the beach come what may. The battalion would go ashore in two waves. The first wave would be 'A' and Raymond's 'C' Company commanded by Major J. F. Harward and Major E. F. Johnson respectively.

0725hrs Raymond Rush and the South Lancs land on Sword beach.

Queen White is a strip of sandy beach with sand dunes in front of the village of Colleville-sur-Mer. The Germans had defended this beach well, siting multi-gun strong-points in and around the houses on the sea front. Manned by battle hardened gunners and infantry with small arms they would prove to be formidable obstructions. But they would have to be dealt with. The planners had covered every eventuality, or so they thought. The unpredictability of the sea had eluded their thinking and the sea state that morning would have a disastrous part to play on the landings. Their carefully choreographed plan was being pulled to pieces by the waves and tides. The assault engineers, DD tanks and the South Lancs were approaching the shore together and not in the order the planners had wanted. The South Lancs would land without the beach and submerged obstacles being cleared and without the benefit of tank cover.

0725hrs and the first twenty-five tanks of 22nd Dragoon Guards in ten LCT (Landing Craft Tank) land and start to engage targets on the sea wall and knock out and destroy fortified strong points. The Germans replied to the Allied tanks and targeted them with mortar and machine-gun fire; and their 88's were brought into action for the first time. The tanks were are already showing some success in destroying German strong points but they were taking hits from the Germans returning fire. In the early dawn of D-Day, the Allied tanks and German defenders slugged it out while Raymond and the South Lancs battled their way off the beach and weaved between wrecked and burning tanks.

Raymond Rush: He dropped the ramp. Bang it went. I didn't realise how big and heavy they were until years later when I saw one. I got pushed off first and went right under the water. He had dropped the ramp in deep water. The boat carried on with me under the water. It didn't stop. I had my hand on a rail and it dragged me along for a bit. I lost my helmet and most of my kit in the water but I managed to keep hold of my rifle. The first thing we learned in training was never let go of your rifle.

There were mines sticking out and we were going in for the beach. My war nearly over before it had begun. The Canadian coxswain grabbed me and pulled me back into the boat. He saved me from certain death. We landed and I jumped off again. I am probably the only one who landed twice on D-Day!

Unfortunately, as soon as we landed, the Canadian, who had been so good and calming, and who had saved my life, took a German bullet through the head and was killed instantly. I often think about him.

Soon there was bodies everywhere. I got some kit from one of the dead men. I'd lost my tin hat and only had my beret on. The beach master was there and he directed us to our beach and shouted to us to, "Clear that fucking beach!" He told us "Don't stop for anything!"

You've got to admire him. Standing there as a none-moving target directing the troops. I counted myself lucky not to have had that job.

You had to get yourself to your beachhead so I ran with the others. A man was in tears in front of me. I could only hear the guns and the mortars and the machine-guns everywhere, and this man crying. The smell of cordite was all round. Bodies were everywhere. Rough tough men were getting hit with bullets and calling for their mums. Dying men using their last breath to call for their mothers, and we couldn't stop for anyone. My pals were there on the sand, dead and dying, and I couldn't stop. They said we mustn't stop for anything and that hurts me even now.

The men head for two houses perched on the edge of the beach where the sea wall ran. There was chaos everywhere. Landing craft were driving over men in the water. Men were jumping over the sides and running through the reddening waves to reach firm sand. The South Lancs were met by heavy machine-gun fire and mortars but, in spite of this, Raymond and the men of the 1st battalion made good progress. The tanks had already destroyed some of the German positions but the move up the beach to the line of houses still presented difficulties. The rising tide was reducing the area of beach in which to work, and bodies strewn in the surf and on the sand presented their own particular problems.

Raymond Rush: Booby mines and traps were marked with twigs with no leaves and were all over the place, nothing had been cleared on the beach. It was our job to clear it. There were posts sticking up out of the sand with mines tied to them, so I shouted to my pals, "Don't touch anything!" Those that did were blown to bits. I got sick of shouting, "Don't touch anything." My friends were being blown to bits.

The South Lancs were a close-knit regiment formed by volunteers from St. Helens, Widnes, Warrington and Southport so everyone knew someone lying broken and dead on the sand. "Stop for nothing," their orders said, "leave 'em for the medics," so the South Lancs drove on. Destroyed and burning vehicles littered everywhere, targeted and taken out of action by accurate German fire, and reduced to bits of metal twisted beyond shape. These had to be navigated. All along the beach front, the Germans erupted with every weapon they had.

Major A R Rouse commented later that during that last 100 yards run in to the beach everything happened at once and all rational thought was gone. Through the haze and smoke, underwater obstacles suddenly appeared. Some men didn't even remember wading ashore. The landing was opposed by as much force as the Germans could muster. Mortar fire peppered the beach area kicking up black wet and bloody clumps of sand and water. The noise was deafening and men were silently screaming. Machine-guns raked along the line of the assault troops and, to add to this horror, a German 88 fired along the line of the beach taking the men from the side.

Raymond Rush: We were up against battle-hardened Panzer troops, all experienced soldiers. We were the Expendables, chuck us in first. I had two Mills bombs so I chucked them at anything in front of me getting off the beach. The Canadians were to our right and they were mad bastards. They had no fear at all. Ferocious fighters.

Eddy Jones was a young South Lancs officer in his early twenties. He had trained with his platoon for months, on the run up to D-Day, and was prepared to go into battle alongside his men. Two weeks before D-Day he was moved to command another platoon and his old platoon was given to a newer even younger subaltern.

Eddy's old platoon disembarked from their landing craft directly in front of strongpoint Wn 20. German machine-guns opened up, rounds sprayed the falling ramp. Tracer found its way inside the landing craft and everyone was killed instantly. Eddy had had a lucky escape.

The way up and off the beach led to the side of one of the murderous strong points. It was a strip of concentrated barbed wire, twelve-feet high and thirty-yards long, but this was the way off the beach and round the back of the strongpoint. Eddy Jones was deafened by the noise of battle and didn't hear the Churchill tank roaring its engines next to him. He realized he would need Bangalore torpedoes to blow a way through the barbed wire so his men could get away from the murderous German fire or he would need a tank. He contacted the tank commander and had him drive through the barbed wire clearing a way for his men off the beach and behind the German defences. In ten minutes, the South Lancs had started the fight to clear COD and neutralize its guns.

Raymond Rush: About half an hour after I landed, I heard a piper playing. I learned later that it was Bill Millin, the piper for Lord Lovat, the Royal Marine and his special forces. Bill was standing there playing as they landed. The Germans didn't shoot at Bill Millin because they thought he had cracked and was stark staring mad. But the beach was clear by then. We had achieved our objectives to clear the way through for them. We'd been sent in first to clear the mines with our bodies. That's why we are called The Expendables.

We had been there for what seemed like ages and, with our first tasks accomplished, we had already moved off the beach. Lord Lovat and his marines headed off for Pegasus Bridge to reinforce the airborne division. There are pictures of them moving up and off the beach. There were no photographers with us when we landed so you won't see any pictures of us landing. You see, it was expected that us in the first landing craft would all be killed so there was no need for anyone to take pictures. In fact they didn't want pictures taken. It would have upset the people back home. The photographers and filmmakers came in on follow-up landing craft.

We set off up the beach and headed for a promontory we could see further up, a grassy area by some sand dunes. The tanks got pasted by the German 88's as soon as they started coming off their landing craft. Bren-gun carriers came off which meant we could go on forward with a bit of support. I looked out to sea and could see the gun bursts. My ears were deafened. We had so much to shoot at that we were running low on ammunition and I did run out. I ended up pretending I had ammo, pretended I was still firing. But I still had my long bayonet, longer than the issued one. I got it a couple of years ago when I wasn't old enough to join the army so I joined the fire watchers. I was given a World War One rifle and this bayonet. When I enlisted, the officer asked me if I could use a rifle. I said, "Oh yes, Sir. I learned in the BICC Home Guard," but I was ready to be a real soldier. The best thing I ever did was join the South Lancs. I brought my long bayonet with me and I was going to use it.

Back at the beach, the Second Wave consisted of the 1st Battalion HQ along with 'B' and 'D' companies. They were met by small arms fire as they landed and the German 88mm guns were brought back into action. The Second Wave of the South Lancs began to take casualties. The reinforcements were welcome. Ray and 'C' Company began to engage the strongpoint COD. It was here, tragically, that 1st battalion CO Lt. Colonel R. P. H. Burbury was killed while directing his battle. The second-in-command Major J. E. S. Stone immediately took command and the impetus was quickly resumed. Several other officers were also killed in the action leading their men from the front. In the first five minutes of the South Lancs landing, the first battalion's Colonel and 2 IC were dead. There were so many officer casualties in these first actions all along sword beach, that the assault on Hitler's Europe was now being commanded and run by junior officers.

By 0830hrs the beach had been cleared, the strongpoint COD had been taken and most of the opposition on the beach had ceased except for isolated sniper fire that continued to harass Raymond and the rest.

0930hrs and 1st battalion had succeeded in liberating and occupying their D-Day objective of Hermanville-sur-mer. German resistance

Reproduced courtesy of Robert Pearson Collection, 2019

although crumbling held out in isolated pockets of temerity. Snipers proved to be a particular nuisance and their accurate fire gave food for thought amongst the men. The battalion and 'C' Company went firm and began to consolidate their positions using the time to brew up. By noon on 6th June the beach was finally cleared.

Raymond Rush: We cleared the beach and I thought, "Nothing to it."
  "Right lads," says the Sergeant Major, "Brew up."
   Stupid bugger, brew up with all this shit still flying round? We were still under fire, but we did as told. We hadn't had a hot brew for two days. Later, I got a letter from my mother and it was a clipping from the newspaper saying that the South Lancs had been the first troops ashore to brew up. I've still got that paper clipping to this day.
   I had a bar of chocolate in my pocket and no ammo. We were re-supplied by the Bren gun carriers who were coming off the landing craft and just chucking the boxes of ammo over the side into the water. A navy man was guiding them in because there was a bottleneck with all the armour coming off the beach. We had made for some outcrops and we thought, "We'll be safe there." The sand was a bit rough, not like our sand at Southport, it scratched our arms and bellies. We got an ammo distribution of fifty rounds a-piece but I thought that wouldn't be enough. We knew the Germans shot prisoners. We saw it on the beach after we landed. We saw six men who had been in the advance party of the 3rd Division, you could tell at a glance from the recognition flash on their sleeves. They appeared to be kneeling in the sand but, when we got closer, we saw that they had their hands tied and had been shot in the back of the head. We wanted revenge. We now realized that's who we were up against. We decided we wouldn't take prisoners. We'd fight fire with fire.

Reinforcements and replacements were brought up and the capture of the town ended Raymond's, C companies and 1st battalions share in the D-Day fighting. The rest of the night of the 6th, and into the early morning of the 7th, was spent patrolling the area. Men were left to their own thoughts and to think on the day's memories and to think of their friends who had been wounded and lost.

Raymond Rush: We spent that first night dug-in in the sand dunes. We covered up and fell asleep. It was a dark night but I could see the sky lit up with flashes everywhere, it never stopped all night. I thought, "When is this noise ever going to stop?". It never did. It was a constant boom. Deafening. We heard the German Nebelwerfers firing all night long. We called them 'Moaning Minies' because of the sound they made when they went off. They were multiple rocket launchers and you didn't want to be on the end of them. There was the sound of these all night long and it sent shivers down my back. They were worse than Stuka dive bombers and you didn't know if they were going to fall on you. I saw a Typhoon go over, they were our dive bombers. So we sat there all night in the dark chatting and telling jokes beneath this wall of sound.

The next morning, on the 7th, we were counter-attacked over and over again by the 21st SS Panzers, but we gave as good as we got and we stopped them. The Germans were that close to us that I thought we were going to get pushed back. Spitfires came over head and I thought, "We're stuck here". I could feel the fear.

Casualties for the South Lancs on that first dreadful day had been five officers and thirteen other ranks killed; six officers and eighty-three other ranks wounded, and nineteen other ranks missing. A total of one-hundred-and-twenty-six men lost out of a battalion strength of 600. The total casualties for Sword beach had been an astonishing 1,200 killed wounded and missing. Officer casualties had been disproportionately high due to their bravery in leading from the front and rallying their men. There was a true feeling of elation among the men of all ranks, and a pride that the men of the 1st South Lancs had survived D-Day and were passing their first night in Normandy.

The people of Hermanville received them ecstatically as liberators, showering them with food and drink and flowers. The 1st battalion deserved the admiration of the country and their county. Major E. F. Johnson, officer-in-command of C Company was quoted as saying, "They were magnificent on the beach, mines, bullets, bombs, shells, nothing could keep the South Lancs back. They were the first British infantry to press inland and capture their objective of Hermanville."

General Miles Dempsey, GOC of the British second army, later paid this tribute: "Wherever I go here I meet Lancashire men, they are acknowledged the world over to be very tough fighters. The 1st battalion of the South Lancs assaulted the beach on D-Day, on the left of second army's front, and gained all their objectives. They have been in action ever since and in some of the thickest fighting. They are a terrific lot of chaps."

The 1st South Lancs looked towards Caen and prepared for the push forward. Raymond would be in action continuously from D-Day until the 15th of June.

Raymond Rush: Later, when I was on Pegasus Bridge, I saw a little girl. She couldn't have been more than eight-years-old. She was standing in the doorway of a café watching us march by and was waving at us as we marched to our next battle. I thought that it was so surreal to see a happy little kid after all the violence of the day. [4]

---

4. The café was the Café Gondrée. The girl was Arlette Gondrée. She is now the owner.

Raymond Rush after the taking of Sword Beach - D-Day.

Prescot in 1920. Raymond Rush's house is the one to the left of the steeple.

The workplace of the Rush brothers before they enlisted.

Chapter Two

HOME LIFE IN PRESCOT BEFORE AND AFTER THE WAR

Raymond has always kept a very detailed diary, he writes about the past, the present and the future. The following, in Ray's own words, is taken from his entries during 2011 telling of his life as a boy and young man before he joined the South Lancs ("I'm writing this in the summer house, a scorching day"). Much like many boys and youths in the industrial North West, times were hard in the dark industrial towns of Prescot, Whiston, St Helens, Liverpool and Warrington, but out of this came a particular toughness of character and a patriotism that drove so many to enlist when war was declared.

Raymond Rush: I never knew much about my father's family, in fact I knew nothing, only snatches of conversation. I think my paternal granddad came from Reading. Grandmother was an American from Massachusetts. I did hear that her parents were plantation workers in the Caribbean. My paternal grandparents lived on the island of St Helena. He was a regular soldier in a Yorkshire regiment. I think she was a prison wardress on the island.

His name was George Rush, hers was Emily Rollins. That is all I know about my grandparents Rush. I know there was a big family, though I never met any. I do know there's a Tom, Alfred and an Ethel. They all went to America, including my dad who deserted his wife and child when I was on the way. So we never had a dad to brag about at school sports or cubs and scouts. We used to make up stories about him being at sea. Of course we had to say he was a captain of the ship. This got me and my brother Arthur into many a scrap when people never believed us. I must say we won more than we lost. Mother used to go mad mending torn shirts and such but she always asked us did we win and when we said, "but of course," you could see the pride and tears in her eyes because she knew what we'd been fighting for.

I regret not being able to call someone "Dad". I could never understand why until I grew street-wise. In my days as a child, you found out the hard way. I saw some big lads gambling in the street, playing pitch and toss. An argument followed and one called the other "a Bastard!". I asked my uncle John what it meant and he told me. I thought I must be one until my uncle told me my dad was in the U.S.A. He said he left us to be with his mother and other siblings. As I grew older, I thought who was the bastard? Not me. It has stayed with me all my life, how could a chap have a family, and with me on the way, and not come back for fifteen years? My dad turned his back on his King and I've never forgiven him. He had served in the British army, a Lance Corporal under the King. How can you turn your back on your King and Country? He left before I was born and went to America, signed a document to say that he renounced the King of England, and swore his allegiance to the USA. Worse than that, he worked for Al Capone!

When I was a kid I used to think, "When I get older, I'm saving up and going to America and look for that bugger who abandoned us."

My mother never got any money sent to her from the USA. All she did was to save all her pennies and halfpennies in a jar under the bed to pay for him to come back. I used to think, "What could she do with that money?" We had nothing. She was brought up a proper lady but now she even had to mend all our shoes. She could have bought herself a dress or something, or treated the family.

In the Prescot museum, there's pictures of our old home. We lived at 20 Market Place. The house was built in the 1700s. It backed onto the church yard, standing where the monument is now (see page 147). I used to climb the railings and the churchyard was our playground, and I can say I've climbed every one of those trees. I often wonder what the old house would have looked like now? They've pulled it down. It had all our lives in it. We were all born there. A steam machine crushed all the bricks up and the rubble is probably hardcore for a road now. The bricks and those trees are all a part of me.

Nan also lived in the house, as did her unmarried son, John. And round about 1930, her other son, Tom, and his wife turned up with the first of their six children. His wife was French who he met in the First World War. We had plenty of rooms, it was a four storey house with a cellar. All of us kids went to the same school together. So now most of my Nan's family were in Prescot again. Ted was round the corner with his wife, Annie and her brood, then in the next street was Nan's youngest daughter, Agnes, with her first two. They lived in lodgings with an old spinster woman until they got a council house in St Helens because her husband, Uncle Dick, was a St Helens chap. So we were all together and ever open doors.

The 1930's were good. There was nobody working anywhere, most people were on the dole which was very little. There was only seasonal work, such as at harvest time, or spud picking or pea picking. There were no machines then, only the thrashing machine for the corn and such. Then it all had to be stacked by hand. Nan's eldest daughter was Alice. She had children the same as my mother and she lived in Platt Bridge. She had two girls and a boy. Aunt Alice's husband, John, was a miner like Uncle Dick. That was good job then and regular, so we never went hungry because we all helped each other. A shilling (five pence in today's money) worth of pieces from the butcher was a meal for all our family. We pillaged the fields round Prescot for vegetables, potatoes and anything else that was growing. Nan who was a good Irish Catholic used to tell us to go to the center of the fields so they wouldn't notice anything missing.

On Saturday night, the Sally Army (Salvation Army) used to have a service at the bottom of the market place. They formed a circle round the big lamp in the middle of the road. There was no traffic them days, only horse and carts mostly. We used to get in the circle with the band and join in the singing. My favorite was, and still is, *The Old Rugged Cross*. When the service was over we marched back to the citadel in Cyprus Street where we sang more hymns. When it was over we got a bowl of soup and a thick slice of dry bread. We went home happy.

I started school when I was five years old. I remember it well. I kicked up all the way but I soon settled in. My brother was three years older and he used to wait for me and he carried me home on his back. He was my horse until I started to get too heavy. I liked school, but not the lessons only drawing and history. I never got top of the class, but my brother was very clever. The teachers were a sadistic lot, never smiling only if they had a caning to do. We only had one male teacher in the whole school. His name was Philpot, but we called him 'Potty' because he was a shit. The rest were old spinsters or nuns and they enjoyed bending you over and caning bare bottoms. If ever we passed a teacher, whether it was yours or of a different class in school, or out of school, you had to salute them. One day Potty passed us on his way home. My brother saluted and I did the same. The teacher stopped and turned to us and said, "Arthur the gentleman. Raymond the ruffian". Next day, he had me in front of the Head for not saluting proper. I got six of the best on each hand in front of the school. A friend of mine got the same and broke down crying.

Potty said to me, "Why don't you cry?"

I said "Ruffians don't cry."

My brother shouted, "Because he is my brother and it was the cub's salute he gave," which as everyone should know is the 'V' sign. I loved camping with the cub scouts at the weekends.

We had four weeks summer holidays plus Holy feast days, but on them days we had to go to nine o'clock mass where we were ticked in the register. If you wasn't ticked in, you were punished. After mass we had the day off. Our day off was spent in Knowsley Park, in the lake swimming or looking for birds eggs, collecting chestnuts or conkers, but most of all dodging the gamekeepers. We used to swim naked. We couldn't afford swimming trunks, and when a keeper spotted us we had to grab all the clothes, anyone's, and run. We sorted all the clothes when we had outrun the keepers. I loved being a boy. I loved the summer holiday. I loved making a tent with my friends and camping for four weeks down the Old Carrs, that's a one time wilderness just outside Prescot.

In the summer we all played skipping, with all the parents, with a rope that reached from pavement to pavement. All the market place would join in, boys and girls and mums as well. All the men would be sitting on the steps cat-calling. We made our own entertainment because we hadn't the money for anything else. But I used to collect any bottles or jam jars and take them to the rag and bone man and get a halfpenny or penny for them. There was always money on bottles if you took them back. Likewise with empty beer bottles, but you couldn't take them to the pub yourself, so we would wait outside the outdoor or snug, that's where the old biddies with their shawls round their heads were so nobody could see them having a sly drink. We would ask them to get our money for our bottles. They never refused in case we told their husbands we had seen them. We would make at the most, if we were lucky, enough for the Saturday matinee at the Lyme House, a kid's cinema on a Saturday afternoon.

We played in the streets till it went dark or until you was shouted in, an inch thick butty [1] with dripping and salt was our supper.

I loved the Saturday and Sunday nights at the old house when all my uncles and aunties came with all their children, all my cousins together. Nan would have the big pot on the hob with pea soup and spare ribs and then the lamps were turned down and my Nan would start telling ghost stories. It wasn't long before we kids were all climbing the stairs for bed. We all slept in any order head-to-toe, girls and boys, six in a bed, fighting for the bed clothes and three army greatcoats.

In the early 1930's we had a visitor from the USA, my paternal grandmother, not a very sociable woman. She stayed with us for quite a few years and she was loaded. Not that we saw any of her money, except when she wanted milk or eggs from the dairy, then we fought for the honour, not because we liked her but, when the milk or eggs was taken up to her room, you was rewarded with two shillings or half a crown (10 pence and 12 ½ pence respectively) and believe me you could buy a lot with that in them days. Needless to say, us kids always gave the money to Nan. I don't think she spoke a word to any of us kids. She was very arrogant and she always stayed in her room.

It was 1936 when Nan took ill. She started with a stroke and she was bed ridden 'till she died. The house was always full of people at this time. There was Nan's sisters and families, cousins, nephews whom I'd never seen before. There were the Flynns from Widnes, Nuttys from Prescot

---
1. Northern word for sandwich.

and. of course, the Melias, all good Catholic names, and quite a few rogues among them. Uncle Edward Byron was a good help at this time, he lived round the corner. Nan died in 1936 aged 76. Just the horse-drawn carriage and the mourners walked behind.

At this time, my mother's cousin came out of St Edwards' orphanage. He came every so often to visit Nan, who was his Aunty Mary, his mother's sister. She died young which is how he became an orphan. His sister died, I think, in a fire. They lived in Bond Street. His name was Albert Byron. He stayed on at the orphanage as an odd job man but, when Nan died, he asked my mum could he come and lodge with us. He was about the same age as mum. He wasn't married but he was a good man and we all liked him. This was when war was imminent so there was a lot more jobs coming available. Albert got a job within a few weeks and so we weren't on the bread-line anymore.

In the old house when it was packed with relatives, my mum, me and my brother slept in one big bed, they were big beds in those days. Ours was half homemade, no springs or bought mattress but bare boards with a flock filled bag. Uncle Ted was good at making things for us. He was mum's brother. Uncle John was another brother but he never married. He always lived with us. He was a character. When he was working at harvest time, Nan used to give him sixpence, about 2½ pence now. He used to go to the Red Horse, buy a pint and make it last till someone put another in front of him. He got paid every night at harvest, about two shillings or half-a-crown. If he got half a crown, Nan used to give him the sixpence. Weekends was the time Nan used to pay to me to wait outside the pub at 10 o'clock for Uncle John, in case he needed a hand. Sometimes he was worse than others. He was one of four brothers who came home after the First War. One of them, James, didn't last when he got home. He was engaged to be married to a school teacher, but the great flu epidemic got him.

One night lying in bed during our hot summer evenings, which they were then, half asleep, I heard what I thought was rain.

I said to mum, "It's pouring down."

She said, "That's not rain, it's the Store's horse having a pee." [2]

---

2. Store was the nickname for a local grocery. A horse and cart made deliveries.

I said, "There's no horse there."

"No," she said, "It's upstairs in Johnny's room."

It was Johnny, he used to pee through the window into the church yard and he was on the fourth floor up. Well, the toilet was in the cellar and he would have to pass through our room.

We lived in the roughest and toughest part of Prescot but we all looked out for one another. Any outsiders came we would send patrols out to see where they went. If any came to our street they would get chased off, especially if they came from the other side of Huyton. In those days, the area between Huyton and Prescot was all lovely countryside. Huyton was the most beautiful village then, all the well-to-do folk lived there in houses with masses of gardens and orchards which, of course, we raided at night. But when Christmas time came, we went to those same houses carol singing and believe me they were very generous. They would keep us there singing for half an hour before they opened the door. They wanted their money's worth.

I had two years to go before I left school at fourteen-years-old. I left on December 20th 1938. My ambition was to be a joiner but when I got home on the day I left there was a stranger waiting on the doorstep with my mum. She said, "This is your father".

The first words he ever said to me were, "You start work on Monday". It was Friday, five days before Christmas. Mum turned away and went in, so she never heard the language I used to tell him who he thought he was. It seems he had walked round town and saw a sign saying 'boy wanted' in Seddon's bake house window and he had told them his boy wanted a job (his boy whom he had never seen before). I told my mum I wasn't going to be told what to do by a complete stranger, but she pleaded with me for her sake to start work, so I gave in.

I worked from nine in the morning till seven at night, six days a week. I lasted two months before I got an apprenticeship with a builder and undertakers. I was to work with the joiners. I was there nearly twelve months before my father found out. He wasn't even working then. My pay was 12 shillings a week (sixty pence today's money) and my mum gave me a shilling for spend.

I was happy working but things were getting harder to get for my boss. Timber was getting scarce but we had to do jobs like making coffins which would be needed when war started. I remember that day, September 3rd, three o clock, walking down Knowsley Lane with three mates. A very frightening sound started. It was, I learned, the first air-raid sounding but nothing happened then. So we were at war, but things went on just the same.

I remember just before I left school, playing outside on a sunny day. The sun was blacked out by Hitler's Airship, the Hindenburg, as it flew over Prescot on its way to USA. The year after war was declared, the precinct in Prescot was then the BICC factory (British Insulated Calendar Cables) which employed most of Prescot, Whiston, Huyton and half of Liverpool. The airship flew right over it taking photos. It was on war work, spying on us.

Among the many essential products produced at the Prescot factory were power lines and telephone cables. It employed 14,000 workers. This trade ad is from December 1938.

Fourteen was the start of my teens but not like today, we were naive as regards sex. Yes, we went with girls our own age but they were mates. There was no hanky panky. We always went round in gangs mostly from the same class at school. We spent most of our spare time on Prescot playground on the swings and football pitches. Things were very cheap for us. We could buy a four-pack of PK chewing gum for a penny.

My brother, Arthur, went for a job at BICC in Market Street and got a green card permit to work. I went with him but he said, "No, go away, you'll spoil my chance of getting a job if I bring my little brother along." So I followed him anyway. He comes out, "I start work Monday," he says. "How do you like that."

A fortnight later I got a job as well.

There was a cycling club started in Prescot. We met at a house at Brooke Bridge that was empty and we rented it at seven shillings and sixpence a week (37½p). My brother, Arthur, joined and he had a bike which he was paying six pennies a week for. He was working so he could afford it. His bike was a Sun with three-speed gears. When he started to work some overtime he gave me his bike and got a better model with four gears. So I joined the club. There was now nearly twenty of us with some outsiders. One outsider was Violet, or Vi, my wife to be, but I didn't know that then. Violet lived at Toll Bar in St. Helens and sometimes I would ride home with her. I liked her a lot but she was eighteen and I was fourteen so it was just good pals. We both liked to do the same things.

We used to all be on the road every night and at weekends. There was no traffic in them days, just the odd car or motor bike. Imagine twenty or thirty bikes and tandems all on the road to Southport on a lovely summer's night; getting back to the club about 10 o'clock and putting the chip pan on for a supper. Buckby in Wales was our favorite run. We stayed at a YHA from Friday till Sunday tea time. It was run by a very strict Welsh lady, boys upstairs, girls downstairs and we slept in bunk beds. There was always a dance on Saturday nights with the landlady looking on watching there was no rules being broken. Any messing about you would be banned for life. That reminds me of one day, I was about to go out when I noticed me new coat was missing. There was only one person who could have taken it. That was my brother, Arthur. And I knew what for. He was taking his girlfriend on a date. And I knew where to find him. I found him in a local field. He was getting intimate with the young lady. They were both naked. I stormed over and pulled my coat out from underneath them. He never did nick me coat again after that!

We all used to meet under the clock on Lime Street Station in Liverpool during winter nights on Saturday, to either go to a theatre or the pictures. There were quite a few cinemas in the city centre.

At fifteen, we were at war but we were too young to do anything about it. When we saw all the territorials being called to the colours, I thought 'Which will I would join if the war lasted till I was eighteen?'. My brother used to talk about it in bed. He was mad about flying so it got me thinking the same way. It was not long after that a teacher at Prescot Grammar School decided to form a cadet corps for the RAF. Me and Arthur were two of the first to join. Mostly they were Grammar Schoolboys. We had our headquarters at Prescot Cables football ground but all we did was school work, English, Maths and Algebra which to me was double dutch. We were taught nothing about the RAF. Of course Arthur could do all of these things, he was brilliant. So as time went on, Knowsley Park beckoned. Me and Arthur and our mates used to climb the wall on Sunday afternoons and went walking in the park. One day we were sitting at the top of White Man's Dam, which was the big lake in the park. We were under the statue of the white man when we heard a roar of engines. Across the other side of the lake, we saw fighter planes taking off. They had made a landing strip for taking off. So that was our routine on a Sunday after that. If we had been caught we would probably be jailed or sent to borstal.

I did start to go to Prescot golf club at weekends to see if I could earn some money by being a caddy. Most members were the elite of Prescot, that is to say most of Prescot was owned by businessmen. They were mostly shop keepers, doctors, priests and vicars and, of course, the mayor, who was mayor for life. I was about to give up waiting for someone to caddy for, when a clergyman took me on. I used to get two shillings a round and, believe me, carrying a set of clubs round 18 holes at fourteen was no joke but, if it paid, why not? A shilling for me and one for mum. That was until I turned up one day and my man had gone round with another lad so I waited till he came back. I asked him why he had taken some other lad, and he turned to me and said, "You never told me you was a Catholic". The lad he got was on the other side, grinning, so that was another scrap I had. Needless to say the clergyman sacked him for fighting.

I was fifteen when war broke out, my brother was eighteen. Things was getting scarce. A few of the older members had joined the forces, and the cycling club was getting smaller. Some of the members had already been killed. My brother joined the RAF. Now I couldn't wait to do the same. He got posted to Little Snoring.[3]

When he got there he thought he was posh. He bought himself a pipe and tried changing his accent. Sgt. Arthur Anthony Rush 1697335.

He flew thirty-five bombing raids in Lancasters and was given the option to step down - his war duties were over and his wife was about to give birth - or he could volunteer for more. Because he made Flight Sergeant he decided to keep going. He never came back from his last raid. Lost somewhere over the channel.

Loosing his brother, Arthur, was a major driving force in him joining the army. He wanted to avenge his brother. His brother's death was always at the back of his mind. That final fateful flight was the crew's last before they were offered the choice of stepping down from operations. Ray's brother's son was due to be born that very same day and the rest of his crew-mates all said that he could miss this one and they would all celebrate when they returned from the sortie. However it was deemed to be bad luck if a crew-mate missed a raid, so Arthur refused to stand down and went on the raid. The raid was successful but on the return leg they were shot down and crashed in the channel with no survivors. Arthur died the day his son was born. Some bodies of the crew were washed up on the coast of Holland, but Arthur's body was never found. Where he was in the plane meant he would have been the last one out. To Ray's constant heartache, it took sixty years before Arthur's name was added to the bomber memorial because he was still officially down as Missing in Action.

---

3. RAF Little Snoring in Norfolk, part of 3 Bomber Group, was the wartime home to four Mosquito squadrons and two Lancaster squadrons. Arthur Rush was in 115 Squadron.

Raymond Rush: I failed to get in the RAF for aircrew like my brother. I couldn't get in the Navy because I worked at a factory doing war work but, by the time I was old enough, I went to Liverpool Renshaw Hall recruitment office and tried to join the army. "Sorry you're too young and in a protected trade," they said. So I went in to work, and I went upstairs to see Jimmy Ashcroft in the office. I showed him the letter. "See this? What am I going to do?" I was thinking of writing a letter back.

I told him, "We'll have to do summat. I'm not leaving it like this."

"Have you tried the Navy?" Jimmy asked.

"I've tried every service. Every recruiter."

"What can I do for you?" the recruiter had said.

"I want to join up."

"Where do you work?"

I said, "Oh no not this again."

"I'm sorry, I can't take you son, reserved occupation."

"Reserved occupation? I'm doing bugger all, only watching a machine!"

Back home another letter came. My father picked it up.

"Hey, that's mine!"

He said, "You've been called up."

I told him to piss off and kicked him out of the house. I was waiting for another rejection letter. I opened it and it was my call up papers. Jimmy Ashcroft had written a letter saying 'This man is determined to do his job for his country and he is redundant to us' - all the bullshit. So I joined the 1st Battalion, the South Lancs Regiment. I was eighteen-years-old.

By this time, a few of my friends from the club had been casualties. Their names are on the Cenotaph in Prescot and Rainhill. I was lucky I came back. The club was no more but Violet was still there. I had grown up by now so I asked her to be my real girlfriend. She said she always was. We got married after the war when I was twenty-four. She stayed with me for nearly 60 years. Our one regret was getting married too late to have any more children, but of course you had to blame the war for that, otherwise we would have married sooner, if we had seen each other more often. But me being away it was impossible. We were happy and we loved each other as we loved the number 7. We lived at 7 The Meadows in Rainhill. But now I am alone and I miss her very much. We were mates until I said to her that I'd enlisted in the army.

She said, "Well, I will wait for you." I made a vow that I would come back wherever they sent me. The thing was, I had joined the infantry which was a risky job. There were times when I wasn't optimistic about getting back, but I used to think of Vi which gave me hope. My mum had lost one son. She won't lose me.

The South Lancashire Regiment (The Prince of Wales Volunteers) was formed in 1881. Its members had distinguished themselves in battle on the front-lines of the Western Front in World War 1, at Gallipoli, and in Egypt, Macedonia, Mesopotamia (Iraq) and India.

The South Lancashire Regiment (C Company) on the eve of D-Day.
Raymond Rush (19th from the right in second row from the top)
was the only man not to be killed, injured or taken prisoner.

Photocopy of the original photograph provided by Preston Museum.

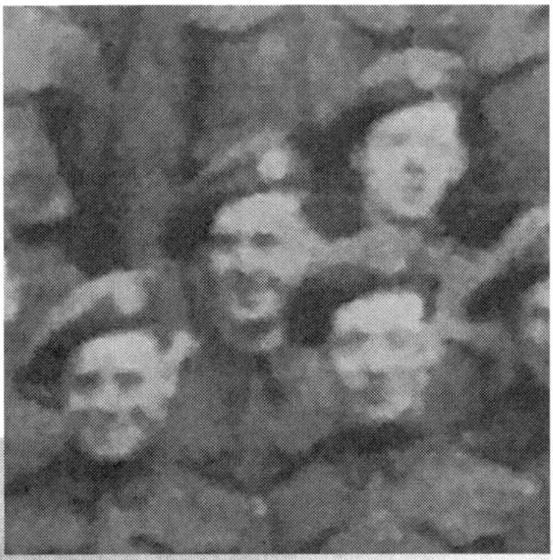

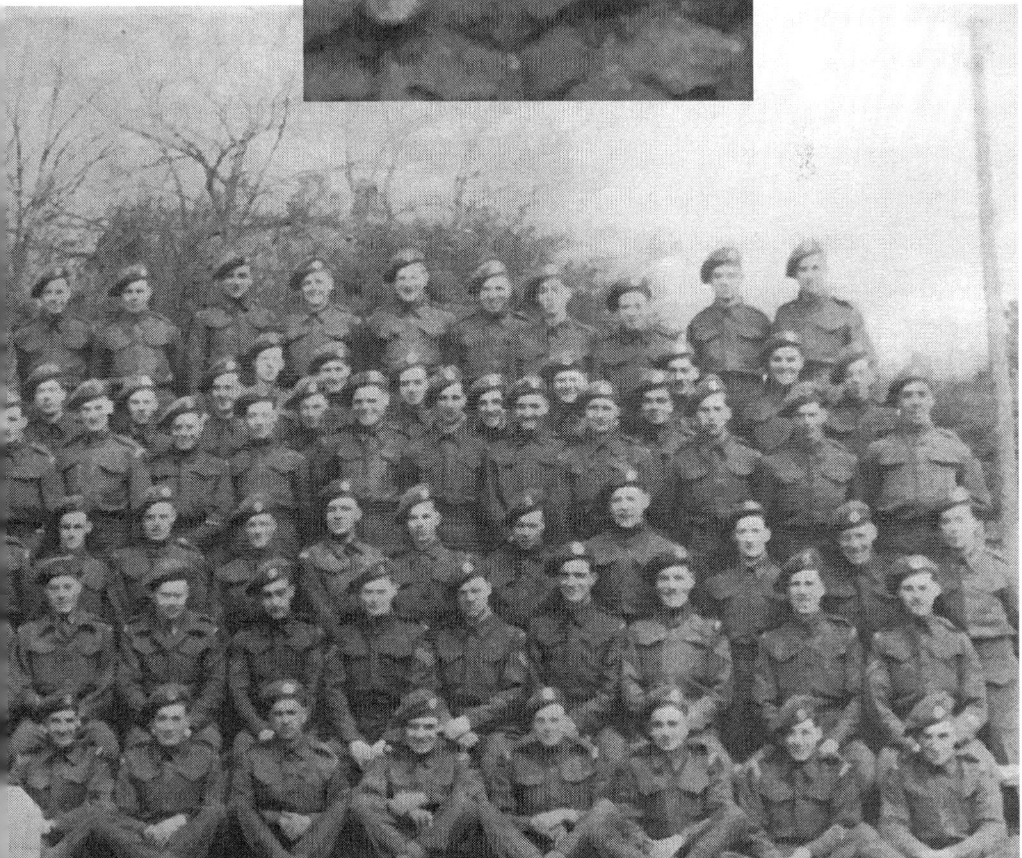

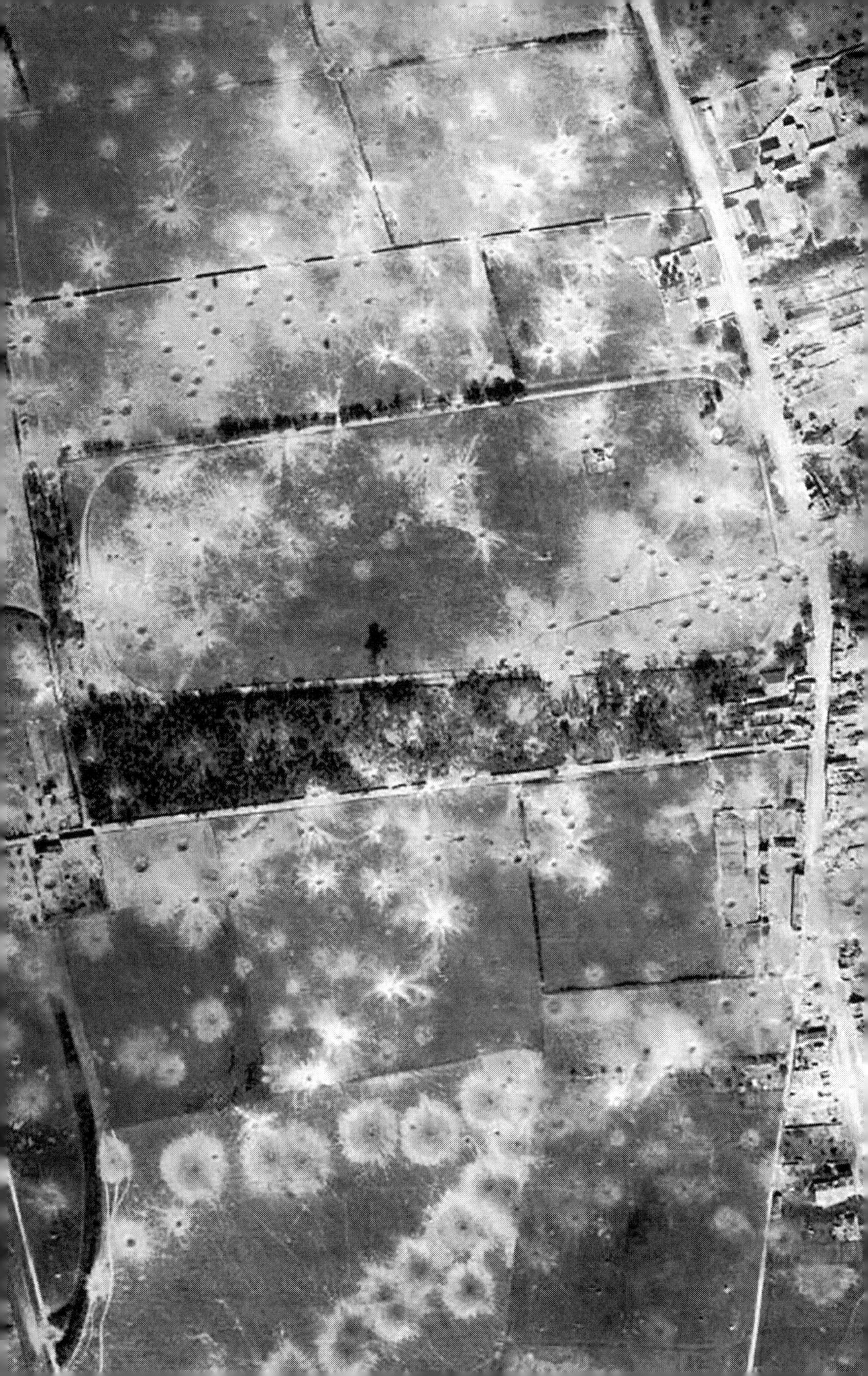

Chapter Three

MURDER MILE AND THE FALL OF NORMANDY

D-Day plus one. Not many slept during that first night in France. A welcomed dawn broke with a pale grey cloud-filled sky. The battle still raged in the distance. To the south, British units were probing from the beachhead to find out where the German positions were. To the east, the British airborne were still fighting to hold their positions around the River Orne and canal, thus preventing enemy armour from crossing them and smashing into the beachhead. Further west, other Allied formations were pushing forward. Stiff and aching, and eager for activity, the men stood-to and waited for orders.

On the morning of 7th June, 'D' and 'C' Companies, South Lancs, were ordered to patrol towards the small villages of Plumetot and Cresserons. This was difficult and dangerous work. The Normandy geography was a terrain of mixed woodland and pasture, with fields and winding country lanes sunk between narrow low ridges, and banks surmounted by tall thick hedgerows that break the wind but also limit visibility. This was the Bocage, every hedgerow could and often did hide a German machine gun crew or 88mm anti-tank gun that would fire without warning. Movement had to be done stealthily. The South Lancs quickly became proficient at moving in and amongst this terrain. The opposition they encountered was quickly overcome and the villages were liberated.

Raymond Rush: We got orders for 14 Platoon C Company, which was us, to attack a big mansion that the Germans were using as a HQ. When I saw it, I thought, "We're attacking that!"

But we took it and they surrendered. We saw the black caps of the SS, first time I had ever seen these swines. They were bastards, arrogant even when we captured them. We got orders to stand down and the prisoners were taken away. We had a brew and some sandwiches from one of the

This aerial photograph of Cagny in Normandy was taken six weeks after D-Day and shows the unimaginable Hell on Earth landscape through which Raymond Rush and South Lancs lived and fought.

houses, a drop of rum and my first ever taste of wine. We sat in one of the mansion's rooms and ate like lords. I saw something move in the room. "What's that in there, behind that netting?" like you see on a rabbit hutch. Bang! Bang! "I saw a face."

I thought, "I've just shot some bugger. I'll be cautious and sneak up on him just in case."

He was dead.

"You poor bastard," I thought. "Why didn't he get out of the road."

That was my first encounter in that house. The first time I'd killed someone up close. I've never forgotten it and it's still with me now.

During the landings, and on clearing the beach, the men took out numerous enemy positions. German casualties were huge in the face of the South Lancs, the first friendly troops these villagers had seen for five years and it can be imagined that they would be ecstatic. These villages straddle the modern D35 road and lie a few kilometres further inland from the South Lancs consolidated position at Hermanville. The purpose of this move was to begin to probe towards Caen and clear German positions in the immediate area. 'D' Company was tasked elsewhere and Raymond and the rest of 'C' Company were withdrawn to their old positions in Hermanville.

The night of the 7th/8th June was spent in quiet contemplation. The Germans, frustrated that the bridges over the Orne were still being held by 6th Airborne, mounted a counter-attack towards the beaches. A column of Tiger tanks from 21st Panzer 12th SS Panzer Division almost penetrated through the Allied lines to the coast. Success would have driven a wedge between the British 3rd and Canadian 3rd Divisions. Raymond Rush and the 1st Battalion South Lancs were ordered forward to make contact with this counter-attack. On seeing the heavy drop of 6th Airborne arrive on the Landing Zones at Ranville, the German commander thought better of his attack and withdrew.

Raymond Rush: The week after D-Day we were moved back to Hermanville. But because it was pretty quiet there, a few of us decided we would sneak off and have a look at Bayeux. It was just across from our base, across open countryside. Somebody said, "It's quiet isn't it?"

There was the odd shell but nothing much.

"Let's go and have a look at Bayeux. There might be some girls. You stop on guard and we'll move over and have a look."

We gets to Bayeux and its quiet for a town, no German defences. They had all buggered off. We were walking around without a care in the world, happy as Larry. We came to what looked like a library and went in.

"What's this here?"

There was this tapestry hanging on a wall. We had a good look. It looked a bit like a cartoon. We passed on and got back to our base. Round the campfire we were talking about it and a bloke said, "You know that's the Bayeux tapestry. It's been there for donkey's years."

"It's only a drawing." I thought.

"It's worth millions," the other bloke said. "Monks and ladies made it in England after the Battle of Hastings."

I couldn't believe it. When we finally got to Bayeux and could relax there for a bit, have a wash and shower, I thought, "I'm going for another look at that tapestry."

But someone had taken it down, I could have had it back to England! It belonged to us after all, made by English monks and such.

The South Lancs were ordered to quickly make contact with and strengthen the defences of the Orne bridges. 6th Airborne had arrived by parachute and glider in the early hours of 6th June and were still holding the bridges and the surrounding area against strong German attacks. Help from the South Lancs would be welcome. Before converting to Airborne, the 13th battalion of the Parachute Regiment, were formerly 2/24th Battalion South Lancs, so some of the officers and men were old friends. The South Lancs were ordered to take up defensive positions in the Forest of Bavent to the south of 6th Airborne in Ranville.

At 1330hrs, the link up was made and the South Lancs took up their allotted positions where they remained for the rest of the day. Constantly shelled and mortared, they made the best of things and, after remaining in these positions that night and the next morning, they were relieved by the Highlanders at 1400 hours. They moved to new positions a few kilometres east of Ranville, in the woods around Le Mesnil again until relieved by KOSB's (King's Own Scottish Borderers). The rest of the day and the following night were spent patrolling through the Normandy countryside. Searching out and dealing with the enemy.

On 10th June, patrols reported enemy movements in and around the hamlet of Le Londel and the Château of La Londe a few kilometres to the south, on the road to Caen. The Château, built in the 18th century, stood amidst carefully planted woodland to the west with a central driveway oriented to the east. Long and bordered by wide lawns, it led to the front of the Château and its imposing double doors. The main building was flanked by two pavilions. Its windows, like lidless eyes, stared along the driveway as though daring anyone to approach from this direction. Any such visitors would be unable to hide from its gaze. Fields that surrounded the grounds were filled with young corn that swayed and danced, golden in the light breeze. The Château's Dutch owners were long gone. Its quiet placid life was about to be changed dramatically.

It would soon become the centrepiece in a particularly violent and bloody chess-like confrontation between the South Lancs and its German defenders. The report said the buildings and Château were lightly held during the day but reinforced at night. The area around the hamlet of Le Londel, a short patrol distance from the Château, was occupied by 'D' Company at 2000hrs. The rest of the battalion followed up just before darkness fell and the position was consolidated. Intelligence received early on 11th indicates that the enemy were evacuating the nearby Château of La Londe and platoon attacks were planned to occupy the Château thereby dominating the area.

As the battalion were readying to move, they came under heavy shell mortar and machine-gun fire. They had misjudged the enemy strength at the Château. The attacks were cancelled, and active and aggressive patrolling was resumed. The men licked their wounds and settled back into the old routine of patrolling.

The next seventy-two hours saw Raymond and the South Lancs remain in their positions around Le Landel. Only about 600 yards separated the South Lancs and the enemy dug in at the Château of La Londe, separated by fields of young corn. They were almost within touching distance of each other. Still suffering a very high volume of shelling and mortaring they carried on active patrolling.

Late on the 15th, the battalion was relieved and retired back to their reserve positions at Gazelle. For the next five days they re-equipped, re-organised and re-grouped. Welcome reinforcements arrived to replace those wounded, injured, lost or dead. Without doubt, Raymond and his pals in the South Lancs were being prepared for further actions.

On the evening of 21st June, the battalion moved back to the Le Londel area where they occupied their old familiar positions. Several strong patrols were sent out to recce and determine the strength of the Germans at La Londe. Any attempts by the patrols to move forward were met by heavy machine-gun fire, so the patrol commanders thought it prudent to withdraw to cover and return to base.

The Château stood fair and square in the centre of the 3rd British Infantry Division's thrust towards Caen. It *had* to be taken. The men were briefed on a plan for silent attacks by the whole battalion. There was to be no more patrolling and probing. The CO said, "Were going in." 'B' Company would move right, Raymond and 'C' Company would go left with A Company in reserve. The attack went in at 2330 on 22 June amidst cries by the section commanders of "In! In! In!".

The men's aggression achieved initial success. 'C' Company secured its objectives and became well-established in the south west corner of the Château grounds. But the lead up to, and the area surrounding the Château, would become known notoriously and ominously as The Murder Mile because of the high number of casualties sustained in this and subsequent attacks. The attack had been without a preparatory artillery barrage and was a "walk in". The Château was taken but, for some reason, the anti-tank guns were not brought up in support.

At about 0430hrs the next morning, the Germans counter-attacked with tanks and drove the 1st battalion out. Without anti-tank guns there was no defence against armour. 'C' Company ran into difficulties almost immediately when several German machine-gun positions opened up on them. Firing was intense and accurate, movement became disorganised and the men were pinned down.

The reserve, 'A' Company, was sent up to help but were met with sudden and very heavy mortar fire that was the prelude to a vigorous and bloody German attack with tanks and supporting infantry. Bloody hand to hand fighting took place and men fought for their lives. Under the cover of smoke, the enemy tanks quickly over ran the 'B' Company positions. The whole area was pounded with mortars and the sound of high velocity 88mm guns could be heard firing. In the face of this fire, the battalion, exhausted, was hugely out-gunned and forced back to their earlier positions at Le Londel.

On the evening of the 25th, the whole battalion was back at Le Londel and recovering from what must have been a terrifying onslaught by the enemy. The next day saw them preparing for yet further attacks on the Château. The Germans could then be observed strengthening their defences ready for another attack. They wouldn't be pushed out again. First they were reinforced by a company of tanks about thirty to forty strong, plus 5 Company's 192 Panzer Grenadiers and a Platoon of Sappers backed up by the HQ. Company of 22 Panzer Regiment, fighting as infantry.

27th June. Operation "Mitten", the retaking of the Château, was launched. This and wider operations were designed to clear German resistance in the area to help the Canadians who were preparing to make a "Pincer movement" round Caen. The attack opened with the Divisional artillery laying down a barrage that the South Lancs had to follow up close behind. Their task yet again was to take the Château. The attack began at 1530 and the South Lancs led the 8th Brigade and attacked first. Not knowing much detail of the reinforced and superior enemy strength, 'C' and 'D' companies assaulted frontally across the cornfields under very heavy fire.

Raymond Rush: I kept a bit of shrapnel that near killed me. It was from when we were counter-attacked at the Château de la Londe. I felt the heat from it when it whizzed past my face and stuck into the wall of my trench. It was still smoking. I decided that it had my name on it. Once it had cooled I dug it out and I kept it with me throughout the War and brought it home. A couple of years ago, my cousin, Ian, had it verified by bomb disposal experts. They identified it as part of the fuse plate of an 84mm German mortar.

Shrapnel that nearly killed Raymond Rush.
Photograph by Ian Sutton.

All the companies sustained very heavy casualties as the attack was pressed home. A and B Companies were brought up and all four companies were now committed, with 'C' Company now finding themselves pinned down on the left flank. They were being slaughtered. Every avenue was covered with tremendous enemy fire power. Ground was being swept by fire from dug in tanks and concealed machine-gun nests. It slowed the pace of advance considerably and, at one point, the advance almost stalled but, in spite of this, the South Lancs carried on doggedly. They were beaten back again but managed to hold on to the wood at La Londe.

The German barrage came down on them and what followed amongst the shattered trees of the wood must have been a terrifying experience. The battle was confused and violent. The fighting ended for 1st battalion at 1900 hours because of the increasing number of casualties. They were exhausted and almost everyone was bloodied. They would have carried on but the high casualty rate meant withdrawal back to Le Landel was the only option. It was now that the 1st South Lancs were able to evacuate their wounded Commanding Officer.

The South Lancs had been severely mauled in this battle. They had a very bloody time against the Panzer Grenadiers and the 22 Panzer Regiment whose Tiger tanks were well dug in and protected by mines and booby traps. They kept their dogged pressure against an equally determined enemy. The enemy had every inch of their ground covered by all forms of fire and his troops were well dug in. The South Lancs had been met by an enemy in far greater strength than was indicated by the intelligence reports. Prior to the attack it was thought that the Château defences were in the hands of a comparatively weak 2nd battalion, the 192nd Panzer Grenadier Regiment. The la Londe position was, however, held by a force comprising three companies of tanks, a company of infantry, a platoon of Engineers, and the headquarters company of the 22nd Panzer Regiment fighting as infantry. But due to the ferocious determination of the South Lancs to capture their objective, the 21st Panzer Division themselves had been severely hammered and had also withdrawn as a result.

A fresh attack on the Château was undertaken the next morning. Reinforcements had arrived in the form of the East Yorks regiment, who had landed with the South Lancs on D-Day, and the Suffolks. A fresh attack by these two regiments resulted in heavy fighting ensuing but after many casualties[1] the Château was finally taken and held at 0825.

Raymond Rush: We got orders to attack the Château of La Londe. Smoke was coming out of it. It had been pounded by our guns and, when they had stopped, I thought, "Here goes."

They let fly at us with everything and our guns opened up on them. I had never seen a building like this. The nearest I'd seen was the Knowsley Hall in St. Helens. We fought all day for it in the cellars, attics, every room had to be fought for.

"Rushy, go in the front," the Sergeant Major told me.

Which was the bloody front? The one with the steps up to it. My mate Buxton was there. He said, "I'm not going in there."

I said, "The Sergeant Major told us to get inside."

"Somebody's shooting at us."

I said, "Somebody's always shooting at us, for fuck's sake get in."

This machine-gun was letting fly at us. It was a Spandau and it was missing us, spraying everywhere. I threw a Mills bomb at 'em and blew 'em up.

We got inside the Château and lay low. I looked at my mate, "You alright?"

"Course I'm alright. This is your bloody fault."

There was nothing in the room.

"There we are. We're in now," I said.

We walked all the way down to the end along this long corridor. I was shouting "Hello! Hello! Achtung! Attention! Cameraden!" This family came out of one of the rooms. They had been hiding so we marched them out. There was some tennis courts round the back that had a big hole in the middle. There had been a machine-gun there but not anymore, we'd taken it out with the Mill bomb.

---

1. For example, the action claimed the loss of 39 ranks of the Suffolk Regiment alone, with over 110 casualties and 11 prisoners. Source: friendsofthesuffolkregiment.org

Château de La Londe as it is today

Château de La Londe after the battle.

Later, the Sergeant Major said, "Rushy I've got a job for you."

"Why, what have I done now?"

"Get them buried."

I thought, "Bloody hell, why am I getting this?"

It was six of our blokes who had crossed the lawn in a group and the machine-gun had got the lot of 'em. Never bunch, always keep spaced out. That's where you're training kicked in. I never said it then, I just thought it. I knew the blokes, I was thinking about them while I was burying them. I put their rifles upside down and their helmets on top.

The Sergeant Major said, "They were good lads."

I said, "Next time you get somebody else to do this."

He said, "You're giving me bloody orders? You'll make Sergeant one day."

"No bloody fear."

I saw them lads when I went back and visited the official cemetery years later. They had been moved from where I put them and I could still remember where I had buried them on that lawn.

I had my best mate with me. He's called John Mather. He was much taller than me. When we dug a trench together he could see over the top and I couldn't. We had the same service number except for one digit. We got to Carlisle first then we were sent to Ballykinler in County Down in Ireland for two weeks to do our training. Then they sent us both to Hereford to fatten up a bit with extra food and extra training ready for D-Day. After that we split up. I stayed with the South Lancs and they moved him to the Shropshire Light Infantry. That was that and the next time I saw him was when I was in the thick of it at La Londe. Out of the blue, in amongst all the stuff coming down, he turns up. He had crawled all the way along the murder mile.

"Got you some food Rushy lad," he says.

He had come ashore with the Bren gun carriers and crawled all the way from the beach for miles, through mud and shit and all sorts, to the Château to bring me some food because he reckoned I would be hungry by now. The Sergeant Major says, "Rushy you've got a visitor."

Raymond Rush and John Mather

I thought, "Visitor? Visitor? Somebody's taking the piss here. Who the bloody hell is this all the way here in all this?"

"A German with a scouse accent," he says.

And it's John Mather. We had a party in my dug out. He was a proper character, proper laid back. He got the glasshouse once back in England for fighting some Yanks. I got away with it because I got knocked out so he called me a crawler. I had a mate when I was a kid who pinched two Jaffa oranges and got three years borstal. I only pinched one but didn't get caught. I said to John, "Don't dare try and break out. Do your time." That was in Colchester before D-Day.

We went out one night to Southport when we were billeted nearby in Formby. We met these two birds, had a meal, went on the fair and he got half-pissed on Irish whisky. I stuck to beer. I didn't drink much so it didn't take much to get me half-pissed. We were walking along the road, pitch black it was. I saw these blokes coming the other way singing so we started singing opposite to them. They were black American soldiers and I don't think they liked our singing so, when they got to us, it kicked off. One of 'em cracked my jaw. He swung a punch at me again and I ducked and he went flying into a cesspit. Next thing whistles were blowing, there were guards all around and I was on the floor knocked out. I woke up and got up. We got back to camp six hours later. We had broken curfew and were in the shit. The Sergeant Major was there with his stick.

I said to John Mather, "And I always knew you were a good bloke." We were locked up in a cell with straw on the floor. We were on orders next morning in front of the Colonel. "I never thought I would see this," he said, "a black man and a white man standing in front of me."

"No Sir, we're both white," John says.

"Have you seen the state of your faces?" he replies. "Black and blue. You're both to go sick and don't come off it until you're both better."

The Sergeant Major was waiting for us. I said to him, "Don't you dare left, right, left, right me."

I got in bed that night and couldn't stop laughing. "Did we get away from that? I don't believe it."

Raymond Rush: Initially, John had been told to work on the floating docks at the D-Day landings, probably for a joke because he was a proper scouser from the rough side of Liverpool. But, after a while, he must have got bored and decided to look me up and give me some food because he knew I'd be starving. He pinched some food from the stack on the beach and crawled all the way from the beach with it just for me, dodging German snipers and pockets of resistance. Thousands of men everywhere and he had gone absent from his official duties to find me. He was covered in mud and muck and everything. I heard I lost John in Holland. He's still there to this day, buried in the village of Mook. It's a lovely garden. They keep it up looking lovely. I've never forgotten him.

Once we'd gone firm (dug in and buried the dead) orders were given that the Château was for officers only and not for other ranks, even though we had all put our lives on the line to capture it. The officers had a nice comfy bed for the night but we had to remain outside, dug in. I sneaked into the Château through a massive tank hole in the wall. I was looking for food but I found a blue tortoise shell cigarette case. It was a lovely piece, real aristocratic. On it was the gold insignia of the Royal Navy anchor. It had obviously been taken from one of our lot at some point. I decided to repatriate it. It was going to my Mum.

The 29th was a quiet day for the South Lancs with very little shelling. The 1st battalion devoted their time to burying their dead and welcoming their new Commanding Officer, Lt. Col. Bolster, who arrived to take over. The 30th of June was another quiet day. The 1st battalion had been well and truly blooded, they had fought and beaten their enemy mostly when he had been at his strongest, but there was much more fighting to be done. They were becoming increasingly familiar with his tactics and they knew how to use the Normandy countryside to their advantage. The Germans surrendered Cherbourg to the Americans on 27th June. The British 2nd Army's fight for Caen could now begin, to allow the Allied link up to take place.

The Americans had criticised the British for not capturing Caen before the end of June. The two commanders, the British General Montgomery and the American General Patton, who commanded the US 3rd army during the breakout from Normandy, were rivals and often clashed over tactics and the release of resources. By the end of June it became a priority that Caen should fall without delay. At the beginning of July, Operation Goodwood was devised to effect the capture of the city. Once achieved this objective would lead to the fall of Normandy and the breakout into France, Belgium and the Low Countries to the north.

Goodwood would be launched by VIII Corps on 18th July, committing three divisions and one armoured brigade to the objective of destroying the formidable German defences on the Verrières/Bourguébus Ridge to the south of Caen. This would force the Germans to commit their scarce reserves to costly counter-attacks. Ranged against the Allies were four infantry divisions, three armoured divisions and no less than two heavy tank battalions with 377 tanks.

Attacks by XXX and XII Corps would concentrate enemy attention to the east of Caen committing German forces in this area. 3rd brigade, Raymond and the South Lancs would be spearhead in these operations in the east. 1st Battalion was not immediately involved being held in reserve at Le Londel where it witnessed the amazing sight of great formations of bombers on their way to bomb Caen and enemy positions in the area. By nightfall, the greater part of Caen north of the river Orne was in British hands. They remained at Le Londel until 16th July enjoying some rest, carrying out a clean-up and taking part in a whole day of exercise.

Eventually they moved to an assembly area at Plumentot on 16th July. At midnight, they left for a concentration area at Hérouvillette arriving in the early hours of 18th. Their task, in supporting Operation Goodwood, was to clear the area to the east of the River Orne of enemy forces. Directed against the villages west of Troarn and the Bois de Bavent, the 3rd division, including the South Lancs, was to advance to contact and destroy the enemy in these areas. Their targets were the villages of Touffréville, Sannerville and Banneville-la-Campagne le Campagne.

Clustered to the east of Caen, and south of the river Orne, these villages in a marshy part of Normandy, had slept peacefully, as had most of Normandy, until invasion by the Germans in 1939. Now they would face the price of Liberation.

1st South Lancs led the attack, starting its advance at 0745. 'A' Company went left, 'B' Company to its right, and Raymond and 'C' Company followed up in reserve. Across the Plain of Caen, the land falls gently away from the River Orne to the east of the city where it then rises towards a ridge of wooded hills. The ground is open and undulating and differs greatly from the normal Normandy bocage of sunken roads and high thick hedges. It is good tank country with small copses and an uneven surface. However, the undulating nature of the plain did provide some cover to the now experienced South Lancs and they meant to make the most of it. The air bombardment of German positions had reduced the villages in the area to rubble and this provided further cover for the attackers as they fought their way along the lanes and streets of these by now ruined towns.

Raymond Rush: I remember being pinned down on a main road near Escoville. Then out of the darkness we saw tanks going up and a German 88 was shelling us to hell so we attacked it. Then they called in a Stuka. We were in a ditch by the side of the road when it came over and bombed and shot at us. They kept missing us but they were terrifying. The bangs of the bombs were awful and deafened us.

One of our blokes shouted out, "You missed me, you bastard! I wanted a ticket to Blighty! I wanted a ticket to Blighty!" [2] A Blighty meant your injury was not enough to kill you but was sufficient enough to have you shipped back to the UK. Some men would hold up their hands and say "Shoot me in the hand. Give me a Blighty!" But saying it also gave away your position, so men who said it usually got a kicking. This man asking

---

2. It's been said that during World War 2 in a typical section of eight men, two would be heroic and embrace the fighting, two would do anything to get out of the fighting and get home and the rest would be the typical professional soldiers who do their jobs, never complain and just get on with it.

for a Blighty was Jackson. I knew him well. He was from Prescot. He sat there as white as a sheet in his dug out.

"What's up," I said.

"I don't feel so well." And this 88 is banging away at us.

"None of us feel so bloody well. We just have to get on with it. Go and find the medic, he will give you something."

Shit's still flying everywhere.

"Where is he?"

"He's behind us. Just shout for him. He landed with us in our platoon."

The medic gave him some tablets.

"Jacko, how you going on?" I asked later.

"I feel better now. I got some tablets. Do me the world of good."

He was a different chap after that. The tablets didn't do anything really. He just thought they did.

But the war was wearing on us. I got a dose of eczema on my fingers around that time, couldn't shoot my rifle so I went to the sergeant and he sent me to the MO. I showed him my fingers, "What's that from?" I asked him. Meaning all the sores on my fingers.

"That's with working in shit for weeks on end, wearing only the clothes we landed in, and not being washed. I'll give you something to put on it. It's greasy and don't rub it off." He said, "when the sores start running, it spreads. So go every day and see a medic."

It eased them lovely. I called it Jackson's rum, I went back to see the medic. He was sitting on his arse. He got some tweezers and took all the skin off my fingers and put some white stuff on them. Bloody hell it hurt.

"Come back every day and have the skin off."

Did I curse him? It took a while but it got rid of it.

We were stood to, waiting for tanks to come up and support us, and I had been standing for ages waiting for the bloody things to show up. I didn't hear this Sherman stop right next to me. The next thing he let fly with one. I was deaf for a week, still am now because of it. He could have let me know before he fired.

Cottages, houses, farms, villages, hamlets or towns, whether rubble or not, had to be cleared room by room, house by house and street by street. Every enemy occupier lurking within had to be dug out and dealt with. High buildings, attic room windows, church towers or multi-level apartments could hide and usually hid a German sniper. Indifferent to their intended target they would wait like a spider, having set his web for the unwary, casual or careless target to come within range. A target was just that, a target and not a person. The shot usually wasn't even heard, just a flash from up high and a body crumpled on the ground, another comrade and friend gone.

German artillery ranged the ruins and flooded the grid squares with falls of shot. Dig in deep, hide under something substantial or you would be caught. If caught in the open it would be disastrous. German artillery commanders weren't without talent and would probably have the area ranged anyway. In every room could lurk infantry; street arcs could be covered by machine-gun and rifle fire, and some ruins still protected families who weren't quick enough to escape the Allied bombers. They cowered terrified as the fighting engulfed their little villages and homes. After five years of occupation that day couldn't come quickly enough. Most hated their invaders. Normanders were on the verge of Liberation and a life of freedom once more. The weak or the profiteers had collaborated to different degrees, but many of the French citizens had formed resistance groups and these became vital to the landings. And many citizens had just got on with life and prayed that their torment would soon end.

Raymond Rush: We stopped by a farmhouse then moved on, most of the fighting was between towns. We came to a village and got stuck, brought up some armour to blast it down. We came up against a sniper across a field. The Sergeant Major told us to fix bayonets and we were going to get the bugger. I was the only bloke with a 12-inch bayonet, everybody else had these little things, like screwdrivers they were. Stick it in and it will still do the job but not like mine. Mine was like a pike. We were bloody idiots, fix bayonets and go across a field in France looking for a sniper. I thought, "Why are we fixing bayonets to sort out a sniper?" I sharpened my bayonet like a razor. It was an offence to do this and you could get

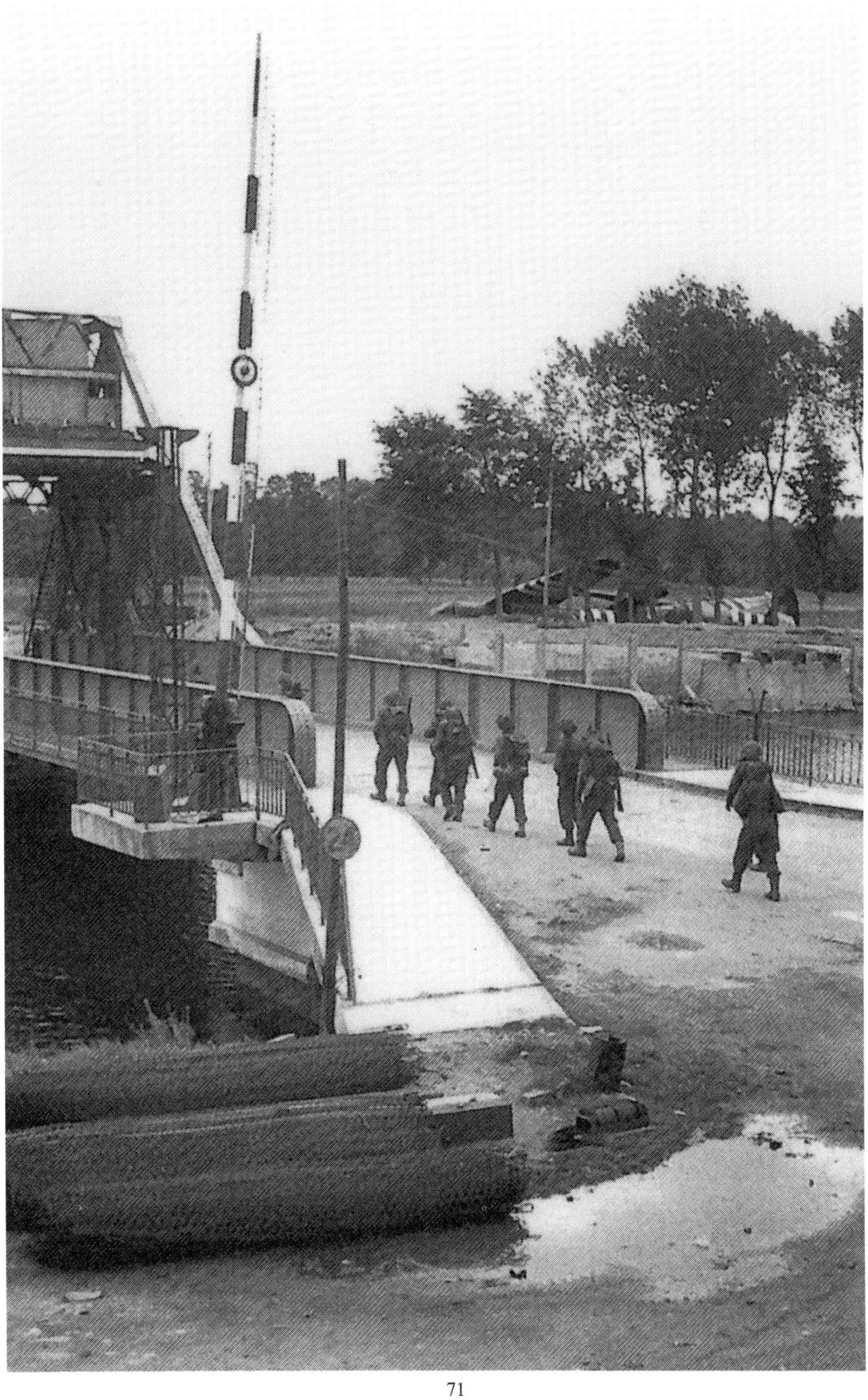

charged but I thought bugger 'em, stick it in, and turn it round. There was a groove along the edge to drain the blood. The others' bayonets, pig stickers they called 'em, weren't much good for in-fighting. Mine was because it was much longer than the ones the Germans carried and I could always stick them before they stuck me. I was thinking about this. I remember back at Carlisle being asked about my kit. All mine was Home Guard issue including my bayonet so I wondered why I still had it. I asked this bloke, "Why haven't I got a proper rifle and bayonet like everyone else?"

My rifle even had different sights. I borrowed a bloke's rifle and my bayonet went click, straight on. Everybody had been kitted out with new kit and I thought my rifle must have been 1914 issue.

I said, "Can't I change my bayonet?"

I was told, "No you bloody well can't. You keep what you been issued."

I vowed never to part with it after that.

On the move, I always had a Mills bomb in my left hand with the pin out with a three-second fuse ready and my rifle in my right. Rifle in one hand, grenade in the other. First thing on contact, throw the grenade and start shooting. We were advancing towards this sniper when Jim Smith stopped, stood up in the middle of this field, and had a piss. I must admit he was a bad sniper though, he kept missing from 100 yards away. We were taught to shoot, down on the ground, roll over to change position and shoot again. We could see where he was shooting from because he was using tracer rounds. We used this to get his distance, fire, down, roll over, next time, bang, roll over, bang. Jim never wore a helmet, no matter what came over. He used to say that's why people go bald, wearing tin hats.

We had an officer called Lieutenant Tommy Markey whose family had pub in town. He kept going missing then would come back to us with more rank. For some reason we never questioned him. One time we were in the middle of it, an 88 was firing and playing hell with us when he suddenly vanished. We moved on and were patrolling down towards a river listening for enemy tanks moving. We were supposed to come back and report it. When we got to the river, somebody must have moved because we started being shelled. There was a Sherman tank at the back of us. It was pitch black but I could feel its tracks rumble as it moved.

I jumped on the back and there was this bloody bloke, the officer who had gone missing was on the back of the Sherman! He dropped into the tank hatch and disappeared again. That was him gone again.

I went into the Sefton Arms in St Helens when I got back home. I used to go there for my dinner every dinner time. I walked in one day and Tommy was there stood at the bar, talking in his posh accent. He saw me and was off like a shot. The next thing I hear is that he lived with his parents in The George pub in Hall Street. I stood outside one time looking at it. I thought, 'Should I go in?' He came out dressed up as a Major and I thought, 'How the hell did he make Major?'

Then I heard that the George was changing hands. His parents were retiring and the son was taking it over. I met him again on a bus going into town from the Toll Bar. I sat next to him.

"Hello Rushy," he says.

"Oh, Mr. Markey."

"I'm Thomas you know that," he says.

"You demobbed now?"

"Oh yes, I came out good," he says.

I could bloody see that.

"I'm retired now," he says. He pulled his mouth up on one side when he talked like posh people do, you know, talk out of the corner of their mouth. He said, "I live in Eccleston Park." [3]

"So do I," I says.

I knew he was running The George, so I let him think while we were talking that I had The Grapes, a big pub in Eccleston Park. That shut him up. That was the last time I saw him.

I saw another feller from the South Lancs after the war. "Corporal," I shouts. His name was Rooney, Mickey Rooney, he stopped dead when he heard me shout. I was there when he crawled up to a German dug out and dropped something in, bang it went. We caught him coming back to our lines. He was dripping with blood, a machine-gun had got him all down his leg. Good lad he was, got the Military Medal for that, Plenty of MM's going about at that time. He did what he had to do and so did we.

---

3. An up-market part of St Helens.

In spite of the terrible difficulties of fighting the enemy in the villages and streets, the attack was successful and against very stiff opposition. The South Lancs were soon rolling up the enemy who were retreating along a broad front. The battalion occupied and consolidated in the villages of Touffréville and Sannerville and, by first light, the men were able to reflect. They had been in almost continuous action or under fire since Sword beach.

Raymond Rush: When we took a village we would round the villagers up. They would come out of what was left of their houses and walk towards you with their hands up. The Germans knew what to do. They knew they were beaten and so gave up. Some of the civvies would leave the ruins with Germans who came out still carrying their weapons. The Germans and French were mixed and had obviously been living together.

"Raus! Raus! Out! Out!"

Next, the Special squads broke into the banks and post offices. They took all the money and burned it. It was Hitler's money. The banks had been running on Francs which were a denomination of the Reichsmark so they had to be taken out of circulation. It was scattered all over the ground. The Sergeant Major set fire to piles of it in the village square. "Don't light it," we said. "It's good money that."

Goodwood would result in British forces advancing seven miles to the eastern part of the city, but the Germans prevented a total breakthrough. The British had suffered 3,474 casualties and lost 314 tanks. The Germans had an unknown number of casualties but over 2,500 German soldiers had been captured and they had lost between 75 and 100 tanks in the battle.

Raymond Rush: On one day I was designated as a runner. Myself and a Corporal were tasked to take a message to Headquarters. It was at a time when there were still pockets of German resistance everywhere. German snipers were hidden up trees and in hedgerows and told to stay behind. They were tied into the trees so they wouldn't fall out but it also meant they couldn't run away. The message had to be there at midnight. We set off with light gear, as light as possible. We came across Germans often. They chased us, shot at us. The Corporal got shot. I took the message off him, patched him up the best I could, and was going to carry him, but he wouldn't hear of it. I never saw or heard from him again. I can only assume he didn't make it. Later on, I got pinned down in a crater by constant fire and the time went far past midnight, so the message was now irrelevant. I never made it to the Headquarters, and I never read what the message said, to do so was a Court-martial offence, but I still had to run the gauntlet back to the battalion. The Corporal had lost his life for nothing. We were expendable.

Early on 19th July, Raymond dug in around Sannerville which had been utterly destroyed in the fighting, only rubble was left of this once beautiful village.[4] He remained in this positions until 27th, under constant fire. Then he was back to Escoville for 48 hours for a well-earned rest. The South Lancs were returned to the line on the 31st. On 2nd August, they were moved back to the village of Sainte-Honorine-de-Ducy, readying for the breakout from Normandy. That's how it was for Raymond Rush in these early weeks of the liberation of France, on the front line. The ferocity of the fighting among the towns and villages to the east of Caen had reinforced the German's view that the British and Canadian forces were of a much better quality and were more dangerous than the Americans in the west and, accordingly, concentrated their Panzer reserves in that area. This was exactly what the planners wanted. This allowed an easier breakout for the Americans.

The link up with US forces in the south took place on 19th August 1944, after almost three whole months of bitter fighting. The road to Paris was now open. These Operations and the fighting in Normandy would be written into the annals of the South Lancs history as shining examples to those who would come after. Thereafter 6th June would be commemorated as South Lancs Day.

---

4. The village is now restored, and is home to a perfectly maintained cemetery hosting the graves of 2,150 British soldiers, eleven Canadians, five Australians and 2 New Zealanders.

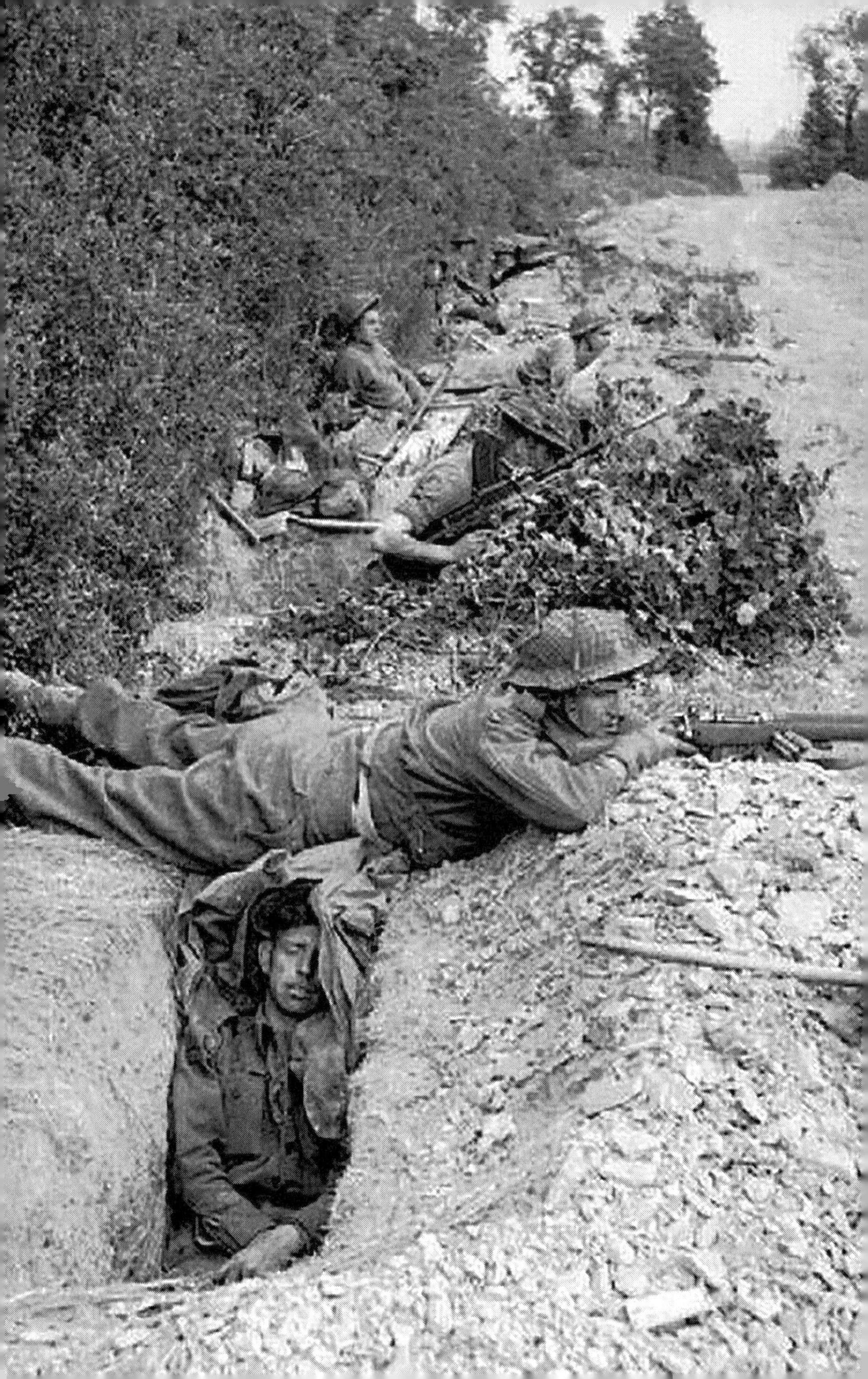

Chapter Four

NORMANDY TO THE RHINE

Raymond Rush: The way we beat the Germans was that they were too methodical. They did everything strictly by the book. We knew they were only allowed so much ammunition per attack, and it would always be the same amount. So you could count the mortars and the larger shells landing. It would be the same every time. When they'd sent those we knew there'd be no more mortars, and we knew what would come next. If they had fired half what we were expecting, we knew they had held half back in reserve and were waiting for us to attack. If they'd fired them all, we knew they had done their softening up and were going to attack us. It happened that many times that, after a while, we could predict what they would do and that gave us the upper hand. We knew when to counter-attack. Ultimately, it was their efficiency that brought them down.

The defeat of the German forces in Normandy made it possible for the Allied armies to break out to the north, towards Belgium and the Low Countries, and east towards Paris and a link up with Allied forces fighting their way north from the south French coast landings. The Germans were not yet beaten and there was still much to do. Montgomery thought that a push into Germany from the Netherlands would put his tanks in the heartland of German industry and thereby bring the war to a speedy close. His main objective was to effect a crossing over the Rhine quickly and decisively before the Germans could re-organize and stop the Allied advance through France. Speed was vital as the element of surprise, and necessary to keep the Germans on the back foot. The British army was ordered to advance towards the Rhine as quickly as possible but there was a problem. The advance of 8th corps and the 1st South Lancs had outstripped the support elements ability to resupply the Corps with fuel, food and ammunition and stores.

British Infantry in a slit trench in Normandy.

Ray and the 1st battalion remained in the Chapelle aux Moines area in the north west of France re-organizing and carrying out the resupply of replacements and materials until the third of September, when they moved up to Les Andelys, on a bend of the river Seine twenty miles upstream from Rouen. There were casualty replacements for the Normandy battles and these new men would have to learn fast. The men thought this a good move and, unlike the towns of South Lancashire from where these men came from, it was like nothing they had ever seen. The town, overlooked by steep densely wooded slopes and vertical blinding white limestone cliffs, was dominated by the 12th century Castle of Gaillard built by Richard the Lionheart who, as a warrior King, would approve of the 1st South Lancs conduct in France. It proved to be the perfect place to rest for a while.

Château Gaillard as it is today.

As the Canadian and Commonwealth forces swept across northern France, discovering and destroying the V1 rocket sites, the British concentrated on liberating the Belgian capital of Brussels and the large port of Antwerp. Once the port fell into Allied hands, its deep water facilities enabled the supply of materials from Britain to become easier. Brussels was liberated on the evening of 4th September by elements of the Welsh Guards, Grenadier Guards and the Household cavalry. After bitter fighting, Antwerp was now open and the supply of men and materials could go ahead.

The British, along with Raymond and the 1st battalion, continued their advance north on 8th September and were tasked with establishing two bridgeheads across the Maas and Escaut canals east of Eindhoven in Holland. Stiff enemy resistance was quickly dealt with. On the 14th, the 1st battalion received orders to move forward again and support the plans to secure crossings over the river Waal and the Dutch part of the river Rhine (Nederrijn) and to advance into the Ruhr.

Montgomery was keen to exploit the reports that the quality of the Germans in Holland was poor. He believed that a fast-moving tank column supported by mechanized infantry could race through Holland, crossing bridges as they went, and turn sharp right to burst into the German industrial heart. A successful operation would, he believed, shorten the war drastically and thus save countless Allied and civilian lives. Operation Market Garden would involve landing tens of thousands of parachute and glider troops. The Market element of the plan involved deep penetration of paratroopers and glider-borne infantry behind the enemy lines in Holland along a narrow corridor. Their tasks would be to capture nine strategic bridges and liberate towns and villages along the route. They would hold this corridor until the British XXX Corps, the Garden element of the plan, could punch a hole through the German lines in Belgium and race up the road through this corridor and over the bridges. The last being the bridge over the Rhine at Arnhem. They would then turn east into Germany, smash a way directly into Germany's industrial heartland and Hitler's factories would be at their mercy.

Raymond Rush: I was part of the British XXX Corps travelling up. We were to take over from the paratroopers at Arnhem. Montgomery had the respect of all of us. Every man was in awe of him.

The corridor was laid successfully through the bridges that linked Eindhoven and Nijmegen and, although British 1st airborne took one end of the bridge at Arnhem, it unfortunately couldn't take the other or hold on to what they had. They were beaten off and back by a greatly superior SS Panzer group that had been refitting in the woods around the town. Small arms, the desperate paratroopers soon learned, were no match for amour. Despite grim determination and gallantry of the highest order, only around 2,000 of the 10,000 airborne soldiers who landed were able to withdraw back across the Rhine. The rest being killed, wounded, captured or missing.

The British XXX Corps did punch a hole through the German lines and did, with infantry support, race up the highway that was being desperately held open for them, but delays at strategic pinch-points hindered the tanks that could have broken the stranglehold on the 1st airborne at Arnhem. All along the route the British infantry, working with the American 82nd and 101st airborne divisions, fought tooth and nail to keep the corridor open. Raymond, 'C' Company, the 1st South Lancs and 3rd division were given the Breda–Neerpelt sector on the Meuse–Escaut canal to take, hold and keep open for the rest of XXX Corps to come through. The enemy, in increasing strength and confidence, mounted repeated attacks. The element of surprise and the rout of defeated burnt-out Germans was over. They had been commanded to hold their positions by officers who wouldn't give an inch. The Germans won back some of their pride. Their flight was over and their arrogance and aggression returned. This meant that Ray and the 1st South Lancs had another fight on their hands.

A mixture of veterans from the Eastern Front, German paratroopers and Raymond's old friends, SS Panzer, were more than ready to stop the 1st South Lancs from going any further. There were repeated counter-attacks all along the corridor and at all the bridgeheads that the Americans were holding. The enemy were also building up a strong defensive position east of Antwerp and south of Eindhoven.

On 16th September the move took Raymond north. The battalion left Le Mesnil and Richard the Lionheart's Château Gaillard and moved forward without opposition to take up positions in an area to the east of Petit Brogel in Belgium [1]. On the morning of 18th September, they were within striking distance of the canal. Parachute and glider troops started landing in the designated drop and landing zones on 18th September.

At 1330hrs, the first paratroopers and glider troops of the British 1st airborne began landing near Arnhem, at the end of the corridor. There were initial Allied successes all round, almost all the troops arrived on their drop and landing zones without incident. The two American divisions were right on top of their objectives as planned. Unfortunately the British planners had placed the 1st airborne drop and landing zones more than eight miles from their objectives. They would have a bit more work to do before they could start work.

34,600 troops of the Allies 1st airborne army had started to arrive deep behind enemy lines and were fighting to secure the corridor that XXX Corp's tanks would speed along later that day. The "All American" 82nd landed in the Nijmegen area in the center of the corridor. All the water crossings in the area, except the massive Nijmegen Bridge, were in Allied hands by the end of the first day. Later in the day, small units began to move south to effect a link up with the 101st who had landed in the Eindhoven area. The 'Screaming Eagles' of the 101st dropped just north of XXX Corps lines and were tasked to take the bridges to the north of Eindhoven. They met little resistance and captured four of their five bridges quickly. The fifth, the Son bridge, was blown by the Germans as the Americans approached it and would need repairing before any armour could cross. The airborne carpet had been laid and was ready for XXX Corps to drive over it to Arnhem.

Down the road, at the furthest end of the corridor, the Irish Guards were waiting at their start line at 'Joe's bridge' over the Bocholt-Herentals canal outside the Belgian city of Lommel, just to the south of the Dutch border.

---

1. The modern day home of the Belgium National Air Defense force and National fighter wing.

The bridge had been taken by the tanks of Lt. Colonel Joe Vandeleur's Irish Guards, on the 10th September, as a prelude to the advance. The tanks had raced forward and, with XXX Corps guns and rocket firing Typhoons in support, had smashed a hole through the German lines. It is widely believed the bridge became known as Joe's bridge after this action. The name remains to this day.

Raymond and the 1st South Lancs were in position and ready, and itching for orders by late in the afternoon of 18th September. All along the corridor, as far as Arnhem, the battle to hold and keep open the corridor for XXX Corps was raging. The British at Arnhem were fighting for their lives. Elements of 2nd Para battalion were holding tenaciously to one end of the bridge but German Panzers held the other. German amour was running rampant through the town and destroying pockets of resistance as they found them. The bulk of British airborne were defending their headquarters in and around the Hartenstein hotel on the outskirts of the town and things were looking grim unless XXX Corps could get to them quickly.

It was the 1st South Lancs turn to keep their section of the corridor open. They were ordered forward to the line of the Meuse–Escaut canal and eagerly took up positions before starting active patrolling operations. Raymond found himself constantly in contact with the enemy on the other side of the canal and brief vicious firefights would break out. A bridgehead across needed to be secured and the 1st battalion was tasked with keeping the enemy occupied and closely engaged. A 'B' Company patrol attempted to cross by assault boats but was captured and taken prisoner. Ordered to force a crossing at the village of Sint-Huibrechts-Lille that straddled the canal, the 1st South Lancs carried out a difficult heavily opposed action against German parachutists from General Kurt Student's fanatical airborne regiment and the 21st Panzer infantry. They were ambushed by accurate and intense machine-gun and sniper fire. It didn't stop the South Lancs and they were soon mopping up these defenders. Not long after, the bridge was in Allied hands.

Raymond Rush: All we could hear was *ping ping ping* off the metal of the bridge. We couldn't get through. All of a sudden somebody shouted, "Get back lads! It's going!" We thought the bridge was going to collapse. It never dropped but I saw it move. I had never seen as many bridges as I did crossing them canals. When we came to the town of Weert, there was this one that the Germans were defending with machine-guns everywhere and everything they had. It was stopping us getting across. I thought, "Run across here? Let's wait till nightfall."

Somebody shouted, "Let's wait till nightfall."

"Bloody hell," I thought, "that's what I just said."

We fixed bayonets and charged. It seemed to us like only the South Lancs could take bridges. We took so many. Others were there but it always seemed to be down to us. I always thought, "us again?" We did more fighting than anybody else. We had that many officers killed we had new officers all the time.[2] I remember Major Judson. He got killed on the beach. Then Major Stuart. He was a good one, big chap, moved very slowly. It was well-documented about what the officers did but the ordinary men weren't mentioned at all.

This bridge we had to take was more like one of our Bailey bridges, it lifted up to let boats through. We more or less walked it. We sorted the machine-guns posts out really easy and we wondered afterwards how the hell did we get past them? They were SS men, 21st Panzers. They were supposed to be the elite. At first we dug in just off the bridge, then we made our way to the cellar of a house. We were on the main road and I saw a Tiger chugging along the road coming towards us.

"That's bloody close is that," I thought. I jumped out of the hole and ran across the garden and jumped into a bomb crater. It fired its machine-guns at me so I dashed back to the cellar. It went quiet for a bit so I got two Mills bombs from the Sergeant Major. The Tiger had stopped and the infantry got off it, so I ran out of the cellar again and it fired at me again with its machine-guns. That bloody annoyed me and I thought,

---

2. The high casualty rate amongst South Lancs officers was due to them leading their men from the front

"I'm getting shut off this bugger." I put the bombs on its track and waited and waited but nothing happened. "Come on you bugger, Bang!" I was just about to get up when Bang it went. It blew the track off. I thought, "That's got shut of that." That was my first Tiger. They were huge things. You couldn't penetrate their armour but the tracks were vulnerable. I just got pissed off with it firing at me. There's no point in just knocking off the tracks if the tank can still fire at you. The crew bailed out and we got the lot of 'em.

On the night of 19th September, a bridgehead was secured. The 1st South Lancs and the 11th armoured division advanced across the Meuse–Escaut canal. The 1st battalion took up new positions at Hamont and the advance went north towards the town of Weert in Holland, through a desolate area of sand, scrub and fir plantations that hid German 88's and dug in tanks. They took up positions to the west of Weert during the night of 21st/22nd and, the next day, moved forward. The people of Weert were ecstatic to be liberated by the "brave Tommies", rapturous men, women and children gathered round to shower the men with their thanks. Outside Weert, the South Lancs came across a chicken farm where they gratefully filled their helmets with fresh eggs.

Raymond Rush: One of my colleagues was Smithy. He was a heavy-arsed bugger. I could hear him shouting, "Rushy, Rushy, where are you?"
"Shut up."
We were on the canal bank and it was very sandy so we couldn't dig in. Smithy was bursting for a piss and there was a tree behind us.
"What are you doing there,?" I shouted. He was nice man but he had a low arse it was always sticking out. He used to say I had bandy legs. They taught us how to live in the field at Norfolk. We were there for two weeks for field-craft training on how to cook a spud. We'd had nothing to eat all day, so we lit fires at night to cook on. We got taught what to do if we were attacked. "Spuds should be done now." They were hot on the outside

but raw on the inside, we still ate them anyway. Tins of soup were good, but I never liked the pilchards. I had some in my rations but left them buried in the grounds of the Château in France. I always wondered if anyone ever found them? I hope they enjoyed them. Often there were no labels on the tins so we didn't know what we were getting. In France and Holland we used to do swaps in the darkness, throwing tins from trench to trench, throwing them to each other. Some got dropped and lost in the darkness. Someone would catch one, bacon! Bang on. We had these self-cooking stoves, that's what you call camping, civilians won't believe what kit we had. We used to get to a wrecked German tank and stop for the night, dig a big hole underneath it and everyone pile into the hole, get the cookers going and cook up plenty of food. It was pitch black and you could see the glow of the cooker but the Sergeant Major stopped us doing it. We used to get an old biscuit tin and a bit of fuel from a German tank, light the fuel in the tin, lovely glow. That's how we lived.

We later learned that there was only one well in the whole of Normandy because the Germans had cut off the water supply. The French locals knew this. So they left barrels of wine outside their houses for Allied soldiers to use. When we went into battle we were given a rum ration. Once you got the rum ration you knew the shit was coming. The generous rum ration coupled with the wine meant we were sometimes half-cut when fighting.

There was this Sergeant Major, Scouse fella. He had his own armoured Scout car. The Scout car was for bringing the ammunition up. But he used it as his own private swag bag. He would cut around the battle-fields looting stuff. He's take anything he felt he wanted. This went on until his untimely death when he unfortunately drove into a minefield, blowing the Scout car to bits and with it his swag bag. All that we found of him was his hand.

The battle of Arnhem was well under way and the South Lancs orders were to carry out offensive operations against the German defenders to widen the narrow salient across the Maas and Waal and as far as Nijmegen in the north. The fighting was difficult, due partly to the bad weather hampering Allied air support, but more importantly the terrain presented flat even ground with excellent visibility at a great distance. Obstacles to the battalions progress also included a myriad of waterways, dykes and smaller canals. The enemy resistance was increasing. He was proving to be a tenacious foe.

By now things were going really badly for 6th Airborne up at Arnhem. They had been driven from their desperate hold on the north end of the bridge. German Tigers were crossing with impunity and were at large and ripping through what was once a beautiful little town. Pockets of dirty, bloody and mostly wounded paratroopers and air landing troops were being annihilated in the ruins of the town. The only firm pocket of resistance was the division's HQ at the Hartenstein Hotel just beyond the outskirts.

From the 21st September, XXX Corps main effort was to effect a relief of the embattled men and its tanks. Supporting Allied infantry were pushing up the corridor towards Arnhem. The Americans held the roads and bridges open to them but difficulties along a narrow road on flat ground presented delays that XXX Corps could ill afford. 8th and 12th Corps south of Eindhoven battled hard to keep open and widen their section of the lifeline and the South Lancs constantly faced stiff German resistance.

Early on the 25th, Raymond and the South Lancs were advancing south east of the town of Weert towards the main canal line. They were prevented from reaching their objectives by German machine-guns and infantry firing from the far bank. German 88mm guns held up their main line of advance and were covering the main road. The men went firm and carried out active patrolling through the night. Having had enough of the holdups, and in true South Lancs fashion, they decided they had had enough. At first light on the 26th they executed a plan to clear the German opposition from the area. They initially made good progress but their task was left uncompleted and the men became frustrated on the receipt of orders to withdraw and allow 11th armoured division to carry on with the work.

The relief was completed late that evening and, the next day, the battalion moved on to Bakel, a small village surrounded by dense forest. This would be home for Raymond for a while and provide a few days' rest. Montgomery had decided to order the withdrawal of what was left of the British airborne up at Arnhem. They should have been relieved by XXX Corps within 48 hours but they had been resisting for ten days. The 2nd Para had been driven from the bridge, and what was left of the rest of the division were dug in at the Hartenstein Hotel. Although reinforced by the magnificent Polish airborne, they had their orders to withdraw across the Rhine on the night of 25th/26th in torrential rain. The desperate survivors of the German onslaught dug in round the hotel and managed to get a final message out before the Germans over ran their positions, "Out of ammunition. God save the King."

All along the corridor, the enemy, intensifying their activities, probed and counter-attacked with increasing ferocity. They pushed hard to retake the bridgeheads that were still in Allied hands. Further south, the South Lancs were concentrating on keeping their part of the corridor open and were preparing to move again to take the fight to the enemy in what would prove to be one of the bloodiest operations of the whole North West Theatre.

It was agreed afterwards that Market Garden was an amazing feat of arms that called on the very best of the Allies' resources, cooperation and determination to succeed but it was only a partial success. Prince Bernhard of the Netherlands was quoted as saying, "My country can never again afford the luxury of another Montgomery success."

There were 500,000 civilian casualties, 20,000 of whom starved to death during the winter after the operation ended. The Germans, in retaliation to the civilian support given to the Allies, denied any food transportation throughout the country. Allied casualties were huge as was the loss of tanks, trucks and materials. The German losses were even greater.

Overleaf: Caen after the battle, 1944.

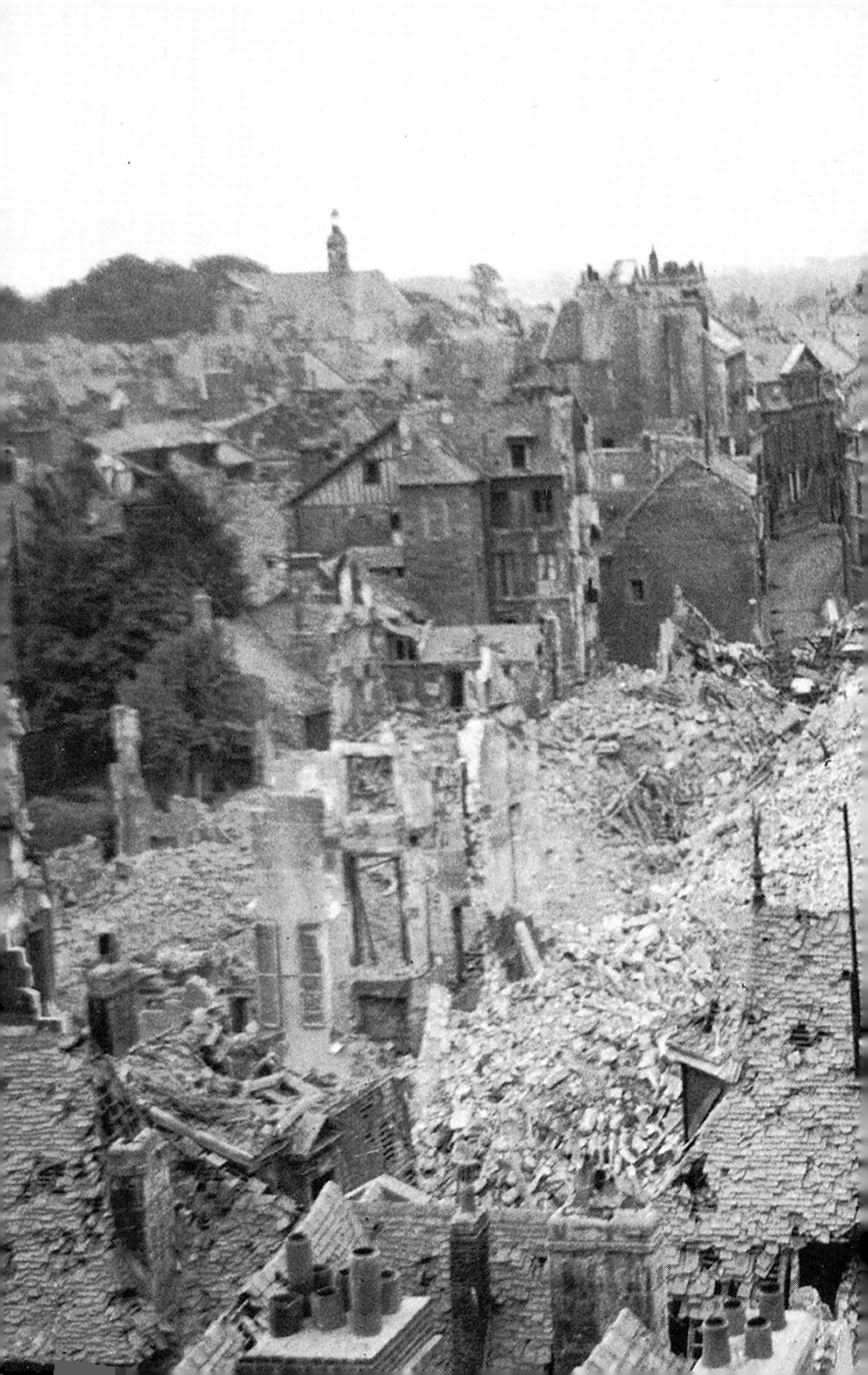

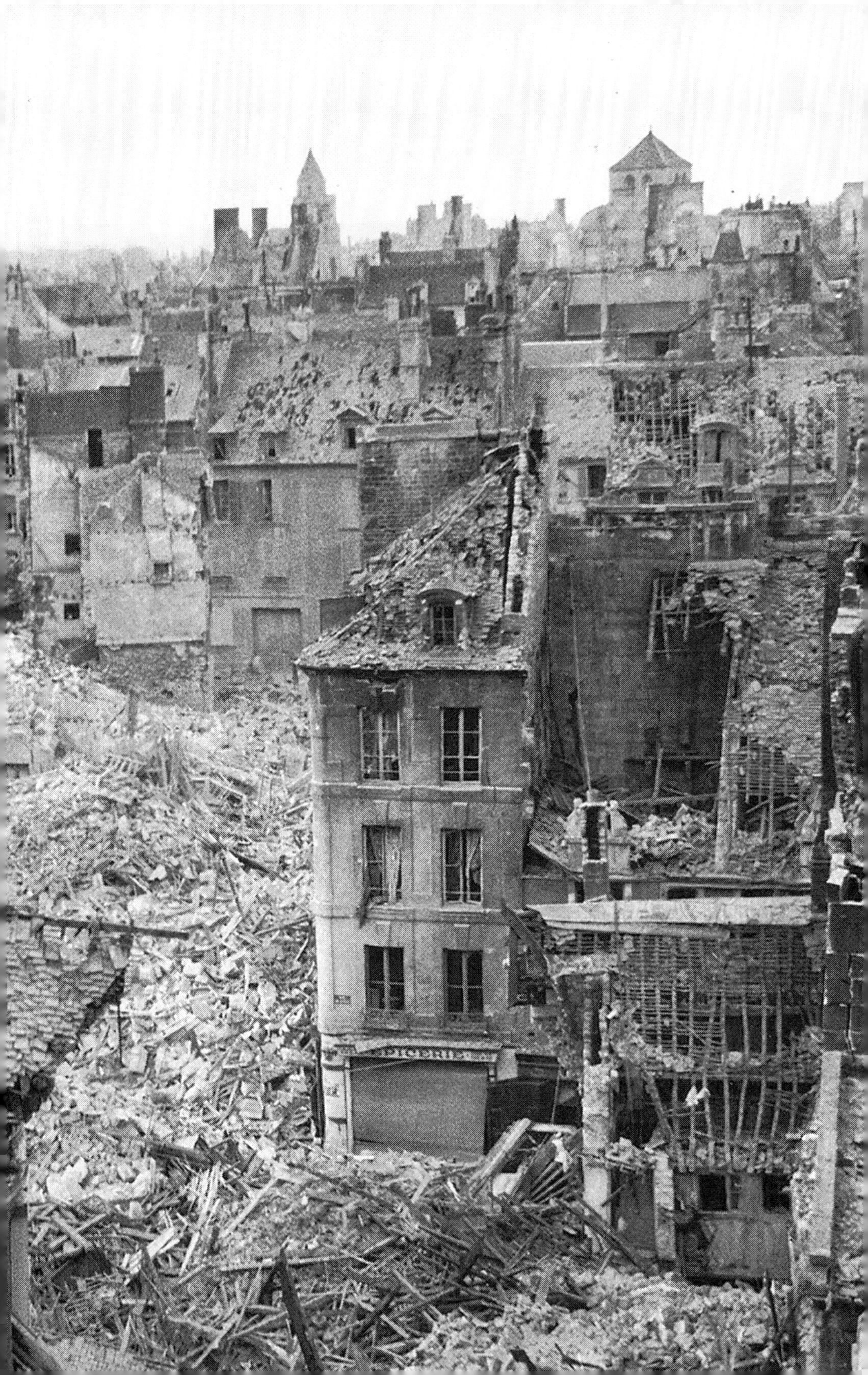

Canadian infantry in Caen in 1944.

Chapter Five

OPERATION AINTREE

"Overloon, it's mines, mud and woods, stiff with the enemy all the way!"

"The concussion had blown me to the floor of the turret of our Churchill tank. I could only see an inferno of burning and smoke. The noise of the shell penetration was horrendous. It was just as though a large giant had torn steel in two. It was a tearing sound that is unforgettable." (C. P. Lamb, Grenadier Guards)

The battles for Normandy and Caen, in Holland during Market Garden, and the Battle of the Bulge when Hitler, in desperation, threw his last reserves at the Allied lines in the Ardennes forest around Bastogne, are well-documented. Forests of books have been written about them. What is not often remembered is Operation Aintree and the battle for Overloon and Venray in Holland. After the battle for Caen, these was perhaps the largest pitched tank battles in the whole war. [1]

Raymond Rush: We had taken Caen, which took longer than we thought it would. It was literally flattened to the ground, pummelled to bits. There was nothing left of it in the end. We moved off from that to our next objective, and on the way we sat down for a short while and watched the biggest tank battle in history. It was surreal. We watched as what appeared to be thousands of tanks lined up in straight lines at opposite ends of the valley taking shots at each other. Smashing each other to bits. As one line was wiped out, the next took their place. The loss of life was incomprehensible. We didn't stay till the end, as we had our own pressing matters to attend to. But the sheer size of that was something you never forget.

---

1. Some of the account and detail of Operation Aintree and the Battle for Overloon is taken from https://www.tracesofwar.com/articles/3180/Battles-for-Overloon-and-Venray. Other detail are taken from Lancashire Infantry Museum publication, *The History of the 1st South Lancs*.

Raymond and the South Lancs, along with the rest of 3rd division would, for the next six or seven days, be up against their old foes, the SS Panzer Tigers and Kurt Student's fanatical paratroopers. The battle for Overloon and Venray is called "The Forgotten Battle" or the "Battle in the Shadows," and is usually only remembered by the men who fought here and by the people of the area. It was also called "The Second Caen" because of the ferocity of the fighting and because it was strategically vital to the plans for the invasion of Nazi Germany.

The partial success of Market Garden and the withdrawal of the airborne forces at Arnhem put the Allies in possession of a wedge of Holland with its point at Nijmegen, where a new front was established, a corridor stretching south for 80km and 20km to 30 km at its widest point. The immediate priority, which again involved the South Lancs, was now to clear the remaining enemy from west of the River Maas. On the southern flank of the wedge, Raymond Rush would take part in some of the bitterest fighting of the campaign around the towns of Overloon and Venray during the 12th-18th October.

During the autumn, the Germans held a small bridgehead over the river Maas near the German border to the east of the small Dutch town of Overloon. Spread across flat moorlands the town had poor connections with other Dutch townsfolk. An isolated place, it had been invaded by France in the late 18th century and eventually reverted back to being part of the Kingdom of Holland in the 19th century. Today it is a modern residential town with few old buildings, a testament to the destruction that it endured during its liberation by the Allies.

Montgomery still thought that an alternative route into Germany could be made by crossing the Maas instead of the Rhine. He believed that an attack eastwards would be the most fruitful. He thought that the lightly held Maas crossings would allow the majority of the German forces in the north to be bypassed. He still believed that the German collapse was imminent and wanted to exploit this fully. But 'lightly held' crossings to a Field Marshall mean something completely different to soldiers who have to clear an enemy who are vigorously defending the area. Taking and crossing bridges that have been carefully prepared with machine-guns and mortars, manned by fanatics with their backs to their homeland, look relatively easy when viewed on a planning map.

German Kampfgruppe (Battle group) "Walther" consisting of 21st paratrooper regiment, the 10th SS Panzer Division Frundsberg and Luftwaffe 88mm battle group and, lastly, the hardcore 107 Panzer Brigade had been in action in and around Eindhoven during Market Garden. With the German border and their homeland behind them, they had been told that there were no more bridges left across the river. They would fight to the last man and would let no Allied forces past them. The Germans were now defending *their* homeland against Western invaders.

The front ran west of Overloon at the village of Oploo to the north of Overloon in forested areas, and over the railway towards the twin villages of Vortum-Mullem near the river Maas. A battle group was formed, the US 7th Armoured Division, the British 3rd Infantry Division and the British 11th Armoured Division. Code name *Operation Aintree* would pit this battle group against the desperate German defenders and destroy them. They would liberate any towns and villages in the line of attack and capture the German held bridgehead over the Maas.

The US 7th, the "Lucky 7th," had come ashore on Utah and Omaha beaches on 13th and 14th August. Part of the US 3rd Army, they fell under the command of the famous General George S. Patton. In action quickly, they attacked Chartres, west of Paris, and captured it on 18th August. Since then, the division had been involved in support actions and had certainly distinguished themselves in battle. Tasked with protecting the west flank of the corridor south of Eindhoven during Market Garden, they had helped to keep the supply lines open from the port of Antwerp for the advancing Allies. They would, in this first phase of the battle, attack the German defences near Overloon first.

Operation Aintree would begin on 30th September.

The American commander thought he would take the city of Venlo [2] which borders Germany, in one to two days. His information had led him to believe the German forces were weak and under-trained and especially poorly motivated but this proved to be much stiffer opposition. The Germans on the other hand were very aware of the Allied intent. They were well-prepared and had defences in depth.

The heavy rains had ruled out effective air support so the ground troops would be on their own. German anti-tank guns were well-placed and brilliantly camouflaged. To the north and south of Overloon the vast stretches of wood hid concealed defences from any observation. Mechanized monsters faced each other across the rain-soaked minefields and began to slug it out. Within thirty minutes, the Lucky 7th had been fought to a standstill by the defending Germans.

The American tanks were soon bogged down in the mud and the minefields. They now fell within range of the machine-gun nests, mortar pits, anti-tank guns and the dreaded Nebelwerfer multi-rocket launchers the Germans had ranged against them. The 7th dug into the mud that soon began to resemble the killing fields of Flanders and the Somme, and battled on. The next day, the Germans counter-attacked but were bloodily repulsed. Fighting became personal as infantry and dismounted tank crews fought hand to hand with bayonets and knives.

For over a week, attack followed counter-attack. There were heavy and bloody casualties on both sides. Again and again the Germans were severely mauled and repulsed. But, on October 7th, the Americans had taken enough. They gallantly had held their line and done their jobs, but the 7th were taken out of the line and the operation was handed over to the British 3rd Infantry Division supported by 6th Armoured Brigade. On the 7th October, Raymond Rush, the South Lancs and the rest of the battle group, prepared for the attack. 3rd Division's part in the operation was to clear the Overloon–Venray area of the enemy, with the South Lancs initially held in reserve, a change from their usual

---

2. The Venlo Incident on 9 November 1939, the day after Georg Elser's failed assassination of Hitler in Munich, was used by Germany as the excuse to invade the Netherlands. The SS captured two British spies a few feet from the German border on the outskirts of Venlo. This 'proved' that the Netherlands was cooperating with Britain and had broken its neutrality.

position as spearhead. This time the East Yorks and the Suffolks would go in first.

By October 10th, the plan was in place and the Allies were on their way up to the start line at Overloon. Raymond remembered seeing streams of Americans coming the other way. To say the Americans looked dejected would be an understatement. Most were wounded and many without armaments and equipment. Desolate and exhausted, the survivors were glad to be relieved. Ominously in this lull in the fighting, the Germans re-supplied their lines with fresh troops.

Operations began again at 1100hrs on the 12th and the devastating Allied shelling began. The guns of 6th Armoured Brigade fired over and over again. The gunners, with deadly skill, fired a relentless creeping barrage. Ninety-two artillery pieces opened fire at once on Overloon and the surrounding area targeting the known German positions. It preceded the infantries advance. Every five minutes, the barrage would shift a 100 metres. Then the three battalions charged.

Hidden in the woods, German snipers had tied themselves to tree branches. Not only were they a nuisance to the advancing infantry but their orders were to shoot any fleeing Germans, forcing their own men to stand and fight. As with the Americans, the German mortars, machine-guns, 88's and minefields took a heavy toll on the South Lancs and the 3rd Division. Anti-personnel mines ripped off limbs and blinded men as they charged. Mown down by machine-gun. Mines blew the underneath off tanks rendering them inactive, their insides burning with leaking fuel. A Dutch volunteer, Wim Baljet, who served with the Royal Army Ordnance Corps with the 3rd Infantry Division was quoted as saying, "A thousand men came back from the attack without arms, without legs, without eyes."

When ammunition ran out, the fight was continued with bayonet and rifle butt. The lead battalions were on their objectives by 1500hrs.

Raymond Rush: We did a bit of fighting to get in there. We were reserve battalion and I think the Suffolks were already in so we relieved them. I met one Suffolk bloke at the back of a truck, "That's Pat Chorley, he was in my class at school!" He was just pulling out. I wrote home when I got the chance, told my mum I'd met Pat Chorley. There was another bloke I knew in Holland. We got pulled out of the line just before the battle, to the outskirts of it. It was a transit camp. We walked in, stripped off and set fire to all our clothes in the town square to kill the lice. Our clothes were full of lice. This bloke came up to me and said:

"Ray Rush, what are you doing here?"

I pointed to my arm, "Two stripes mate, and Corporal to you."

I can never think of his name. I always called him Whitefield. He lived down nearby Tesco's in Prescot. Every week I'd see him shopping in Prescot. "Hello, still here then?"

"Still here." That's all the conversation we ever had. They were the only two I met who I knew.

When Raymond entered the town there wasn't much of it left. German snipers held out in the church tower. They were a nuisance and would have to be dealt with. Allied bombers dropped incendiaries on the church and the remaining Germans dynamited what was left before finally evacuating. Evidence of atrocities on Allied prisoners were evident in the town square. Other captured Allied prisoners were found kneeling, shot in the backs of their heads.

Raymond Rush: We came to a barn and went inside to clear it. To this day this haunts me. It's one of the things I can't get out of my head even after 75 years, it brings the nightmares that I still have. The SS had been there and had nailed the genitals of some prisoners onto one of the walls, and other mutilated parts. Churchill said, "If you are going through Hell. Keep going." That's where we were. And that's what we did. We kept going.

This was a very bloody business and the enemy would be made to pay. The South Lancs received orders to clear a wooded area at the southern end of Overloon town. They completed and secured their objectives by nightfall. There had been some opposition but it wasn't as heavy as the men had expected and, without hindrance, they dug in once more for the night. The next morning after a fitful night's sleep they continued the advance, but it slowed when they became on the receiving end of concentrated Nebelwerfer fire and found themselves moving through minefields. Early that afternoon, they went firm and allowed the KOSB (King's Own Scottish Borderers) to pass through their lines.

Raymond Rush: There was a period of quiet in the battle. We broke into a farm house to take cover and re-distribute our ammunition. There was a piano in there. My mother had a piano, she couldn't read music but she could play any tune. We'd have family gatherings every Friday and she'd play there. I thought I'd have a go at this piano. I started playing it and for a short while I felt I was back at home. But the calmness was soon broken by the sound of machine-gun and mortar fighter. I ignored the fighting going on outside and made sure I'd finished the tune first. Then I stood up and said, "Now, I'm ready." And I joined in the fight.

Early on 14th October, the South Lancs received orders to move again. They were ordered to take up positions to the east of Overloon and prepare for an assault on the little town of Halfweg.

By 1800hrs, the area was secure and South Lancs had taken one-hundred-and-two prisoners, an astonishing eighty-three of whom were taken by Raymond's 'C' Company. It hadn't been easy fighting. They met fierce enemy opposition the whole time and unmarked minefields were everywhere.

On the morning of the 15th, after a day of heavy fighting, the South Lancs allowed the 11th Armoured Division to pass their positions and cross the cleared areas they had paid for so dearly. The 8th infantry brigade received new orders to continue with their advance and mount an attack on Venray town itself. The attack started early on 16th. South Lancs' brigade companions, the Suffolks and East Yorks, led the way leaving the South Lancs in reserve. As expected, the enemy resisted fiercely and the thick woodland and minefields made progress difficult.

Raymond Rush: We got to Venray woods and I'm haunted by this as well. We patrolled in during the night to take up our positions. We couldn't see. It was pitch dark but we knew we were walking over the dead bodies of fallen comrades killed earlier in the fighting. They were everywhere. Some of these memories never leave me. It was horrible. All day and all night there is the stench of rotting bodies, both human and animal; bloated cows in the field, rotting corpses of men from previous battles. There was no time to bury them. You were still in the battle.

The weather was awful. We had greatcoats and capes. I was in a slit trench and "Bang!" a shell went off right by my ear. That was when Peter Coolie, he was only a few yards away in his trench, shouted back to me, "Rushy, are you going back for some bloody food?"

"Where is it?"

"In a trench, only just over there."

"Go on then I'll go."

Anyroad, I crawled out in the slutch.[3] Trees were crashing down all round me from the shelling and mortars. I was brushing sparks off me. I got to the trench, it had a cover over it. I couldn't see anything inside so I felt for the tins, sardines, pilchards. I was after the beef and the stew. So I gets all these tins and stuffs them in my knapsack. I started to crawl back again and heard this terrific bang. It was a mortar shell and I'm blind and half buried. I lay there, my heart going like mad. The tins were all buried so I used my bayonet to dig them out. I don't know how long it took me. All I could hear was, "Rushy! Rushy!" He was shouting for me.

"Bloody hell, Pete, shut up."

I crawled over to where he was in his trench and puts my hand inside and he grabs it. I said: "Oh, thank God you're all right."

"I'm hit," he said.

"It's only a flesh wound, you'll be alright."

A flesh wound? There was plenty of flesh, I could feel it. He flaked out. I think because I had got to him. He'd lost his leg. There was only a stump left. I shouted for the medics. They were in no hurry, being heavily bombarded as well. "For fuck's sake! He's dying here!"

---

3. *Anyroad* is a northern word for *Anyway*. *Sluch* is a northern word for *slimy wet mud*.

Pete said, "No I'm not. No I'm not."

We only had penicillin tablets, no morphine like the Yanks, so I couldn't do much. I got him out of the trench and the medics carried him away in my overcoat, I only had my battle dress then. I was freezing. I felt this sticky blood and bits of bone, bloody hell it scared me that.

The Sergeant comes over. "What's up?"

"What's up? Where the bloody hell have you been? I've been here half an hour, and bleeding to death," I said.

"Where are you hurt?" He says.

"Not me, I'm not hurt, Peter was bleeding to death. They've whipped him off, and he's got no legs on.

"You lying bugger."

Pete was from Widnes and I met him after the war. He had a tin leg by then. I had a job working shift work, working two till ten in the brewery in St Helens just after the war. My missus worked in the Co-op in Church Street. She was manageress. I called in after work one time in the afternoon. As soon as she saw me she ran to the door and shut it and pulled the blind down.

"You can't come in yet, I've got somebody in," she said smiling at me.

"Open the bloody door! It's me."

She opened the door and there he was grinning.

"You bloody bugger," I said.

We went in every pub in St Helens. Now I'm not used to beer. I'd never had a pint before in my life except the one before Normandy. I looked at Peter with that daft grin on his face. "Get it supped," he says, "If you don't sup it I'll pour it down you." Guinness mix it was. Bloody lovely drink.

He could drink. I said to him, "Where are you putting that lot?"

We spent the day together, it was a Sunday. He had two cracking sisters who were barmaids in the pubs in town. We walked home in the early hours and he took me home. Nobody up waiting for me. The table was laid with a plate of sandwiches and a bottle of Guinness. I said to my mum later, "What's the idea of a plate of sandwiches and Guinness."

"You need it son," she says, "You need it."

I always said I'd keep in touch with Pete. I never did.

The battle had entered a new phase. 1st South Lancs orders were now to be in reserve as a quick reaction force and fill a support role to be ready for every eventuality. Late on the 18th September they were ordered to seize the southern part of Venray. The town was believed to have been abandoned. At 0645hrs on 18th, and without attracting any enemy attention, the attack started. By 0730, and with its objectives secured, the battalion went "firm" (consolidate their position) in the town. On leaving the town at 0830hrs, the 1st battalion came under heavy artillery fire and sustained heavy casualties.

By 0920hrs, the 1st battalion had again secured its objectives and, after consolidating their positions, they began to dig in. The final capture of Venray ended this part of the Aintree operation. This meant that the enemy further south of the town could now be dealt with.

Raymond Rush and the 1st battalion remained in the ruined Venray for several days as an occupying force. The surviving townspeople could at last crawl from their hiding places in cellars from where, terrified, they had witnessed the fighting. The townspeople poured out as they had in every town and village the Allies had liberated in Holland. They decked their rubble strewn and broken streets with orange flags, ribbons, cloth, anything orange, their symbol of nationhood. They brought out and hung, where they could, carefully hidden portraits of their beloved Queen Wilhelmina, the Princess Juliana and Crown Prince Bernhard. Children appeared as if from nowhere to beg cigarettes and chocolate from the battle-worn but victorious Tommys, scolded by their elders to remember their manners. "Remember your manners, children. Dutch kids don't scrounge." Everyone wore a bright orange item of clothing that contrasted starkly with the grim, grey all around them.

The Dutch resistance began to get organised and sent people out to round up the hated collaborators. They shared intelligence on German positions and strengths with the Allied intelligence officers. German stragglers were rounded up and, relieved the fighting had stopped, resigned themselves to their captivity. Raymond and his mates made themselves as comfortable as they could. The townspeople welcomed them as sons.

Raymond Rush: I was on sentry duty on my own in a trench with the Bren. My job was to watch for any Germans coming back into the town. I didn't know who she was or where she came from, I think she might have come from the jewellers that was behind me, maybe from one of the cellars. She jumped into the trench with me and kept me company all night long. She had this fur coat on that she wrapped round us. I never wanted that night to end.

The South Lancs carried out more active patrolling probing towards the Maas and the surrounding area until they received orders to move back to Overloon for a well-earned rest and training. On the 26th, the 2nd Royal Warwicks took over relief in Venray and occupied the South Lancs positions. Although there was still a great deal of enemy shelling, the South Lancs spent a much welcomed eight days in Overloon to rest and reorganise.

Raymond Rush: I don't know who dropped the Sten gun. We were in a house in a village just outside Overloon. We had this table in the middle of a wash house with all our kit on it. We were cleaning everything while we could. We'd been in action and the Sergeant said, "Right lads, get your weapons cleaned up. Anybody got any souvenirs?"

I said, "I've got a 38 revolver." It was like a Luger only smaller. Nice pistol. Somebody said, "Let's try it? Let's have a go?"

"Nobody's touching that," I said. "You're not firing it."

He snatched it off me. I had a Sten gun as my personal weapon. As an N.C.O. Corporal I had the choice of a Sten Gun or a Tommy Gun so I picked the Sten. You had to be careful with it, it could go off easy and, on automatic, it would empty the magazine in seconds.

The next thing the lads have snatched for the 38 and were scrapping for it. It went up in the air and my Sten fell onto the table. It went off and sprayed rounds all round the room. By a bloody miracle it missed everybody.

"What happened, what happened?"

The doors burst open and everyone runs in thinking the Germans were counter-attacking.

"Where's the enemy? Where's the enemy?" But it was only my Sten gun. I lost my Corporal tapes because of that and got put on a charge.

Post-war correspondence between the Officers of 1st South Lancs and the town of Overloon officials spoke warmly and affectionately of the relationship between the 1st South Lancs and the people of the town. The people of Overloon would be eternally grateful to the 1st battalion for the sacrifices they made during those terrible weeks in October 1944. The battalion was commemorated in the town during a ceremony held after the war when a shield badge of 1st South Lancs was presented to the Burgomaster by the CO. The war brought a lasting friendship. It was noted that the battalion had left many of its officers and men as permanent guests resting in the cemeteries. They would always be looked after as sons. Battered and desolate, the town's little church had sheltered many South Lancs men from the German onslaught and would be rebuilt. A new Overloon has risen out of the ashes of war and the town even now reinforces its brotherhood with the 1st South Lancs.

Raymond Rush: Before we got to Overloon things seemed a bit quiet. We got to a big place called Vier. It had a Cathedral and this big tower. They were firing at us from the top of this tower, so one of our 25-pounder guns soon got it. It blew the top off it. There was no firing after that.

It was a nice town but we didn't know who was in front of us. We were picking up German stragglers all the time but there was still plenty of them. Their machine-guns were everywhere. All the Germans seemed to have machine-guns, Schmeissers and Spandau. The Spandau had an echo sound when it let fly with bursts of firing and that sound you never forgot. One after the other would start up. Their Moaning Minnies were worst, I shit myself when I heard them. You could hear them moving them about into position. Then they'd start up one after the other and they'd come down like on a blanket and you're thinking, don't hit me, don't hit me.

Peter Haar writes: "Although the fighting near Overloon and Venray was labelled to be amongst the fiercest fighting in the entire European Theatre of Operations, the battle was more or less forgotten. It was called "The Second Caen" by the troops of the 3rd Infantry Division and the 11th Armoured Division. These divisions had slugged it out for months with the Germans in Normandy.
The British suffered 1,426 casualties, among whom 753 dead and missing. 3rd Infantry Division lost 400 dead and 11th Armoured Division lost 273 killed. 281 of them rest in Overloon war cemetery.

The German losses are estimated at 600. Most of them were reburied after the war on the military cemetery of nearby Ysselsteyn. On October 12th, the first day of the British assault, 147 were taken prisoner. The German Parachute battalion "Paul" lost 402 men. 81 killed, 80 wounded and 241 missing, from whom 102 were taken prisoner.

The losses of the Dutch civilian population are also difficult to determine precisely. A number of 300 dead is given. Overloon and the rest of the area was evacuated but some people stayed behind and hid in their cellars.

The bloody fighting at Overloon, the Molenbeek, Venray and the surrounding villages and woods can be seen as a defensive success for the Germans. Terrain was slowly given up and heavy casualties were inflicted. The Germans fought with their backs against the Maas and they were told that the bridges were blown up. Many German soldiers, even at this stage of the war, believed that they still could win or gain a favourable peace." [4]

---

4. Published on www.tracesofwar.com/articles/3180/Battles-for-Overloon-and-Venray. 12/2/14.

British Cromwell tanks crossing a Bailey bridge built over the Orne River.

Durham Light Infantry with a wrecked German Tiger tank, 28 June 1944.

Chapter Six

THE WINTER OF 1944

October turned to November and the South Lancs were to face the wettest and coldest winter for decades. Many friends and comrades had been lost in the battles for Overloon and Venray. The towns had been liberated from tyranny and all the men who were left believed that the loss of so many good men for the freedom it had given these Dutch people was a fair trade.

On the 4th November, the South Lancs moved to near the 'riool' or sewage reservoirs to the east of Venray to relieve the exhausted Royal Ulster Rifles. A period of intense, active and aggressive patrolling followed, contact after contact and short sharp exchanges of small arms fire spread along the railway lines that ran to the east of Venray. This area of German forward defensive positions had elements of the German battle groups that Raymond and the South Lancs had been fighting around Overloon and Venray.

Raymond Rush: I lay in a hole for days, I couldn't get out with all the firing at us. A bloke outside of my hole shouted from somewhere, "Come on out, there's nobody here now and the firing's stopped."

As soon as you showed yourself they let fly again. The Dutch people were very generous, they didn't have much but they said we could take anything we wanted, really generous people. When we came to Venray there were some lovely shops just like back home, musical shops and jewellery shops. No one took anything, no one stole from these people. We were warned though not to touch anything because of the booby traps. There were shoe boxes thrown everywhere.

"Give it a kick," someone shouted, "See what it is."

The first time someone did that a bloke died. They were push-down mines, move the box and bang. We lost two Lieutenants in a month doing exactly the same as that, Boom! Foot off.

We would go into a house and we were allowed to eat anything we found. "Come in here lads and have a look at this." Big demijohns full of pickled carrots and potatoes. Everything was pickled in brine to preserve it. It would be bloody gorgeous, imagine fresh pickled everything. I was starving and would eat anything. Imagine a platoon going into a house, "Right lads," says the Sergeant. "This is your billet now."

Our platoon in one house, another in the next and you have to look after each other. There were booby traps and trip wires all over the bloody place. The new recruit Sergeants, fresh from England, didn't know anything, "Don't touch anything," they would say.

"Oh we know that." They thought us bloody stupid. They came fresh from England as know it alls. We gets set up. He says, "Don't light any fires. They will see the smoke coming from the chimneys."

We got a bit of lamb. "How are we going to cook this then?"

Some bright spark with his stripes, really new and white, said, "Your boy scouts upbringing should kick in."

We called him 'Cookie' after that. He got buggered about all up and down the place. We'd shoot a pig or some game and tell him to cook it. He became the cook. You see, over there, rank never came into it. You said what you thought.

The Germans were carrying out aggressive patrolling activities in this area so there were, especially at night, brisk and bloody violent outbreaks of fighting as patrols came across each other in the dark. This was terrifying work but the South Lancs seemed to be getting the upper hand of the exchanges because the enemy's activity was noticed to be decreasing. More reconnaissance patrolling was carried out, observation posts and listening posts were set up and much information and intelligence was gathered on the enemy's numbers, strength and his defensive capabilities.

Raymond Rush: They were arrogant buggers. We would watch them smoking cigars, talking away. I don't know how we were supposed to be gathering information, we couldn't understand a bloody word they were saying. We were near the River Maas just outside Venray. I was patrol commander on a listening patrol.

The idea was we would get into position so that we could hear the Germans and gather intelligence about them. We crawled from our trenches down to the river, quietly settle down. No smoking allowed. It was winter and there was snow up to our heads. The Germans were across the river. It was a scream this was, on a listening patrol and none of us could speak or understand German!

On another patrol, with me again as patrol commander, we were told to snatch some prisoners. Don't kill them all. They said, "Right, night patrol tonight."

"Oh no, watch my name come up again," and it came up.

"Where are we going?" I asked.

"To where I say."

That's what it was like, you do as you're told. We set up an ambush and the heavens opened up, just outside Venray it was.

"You have to listen to tell us what they're doing and where they're going, just guess if you don't understand them and, at first light, make your way back."

What we did do was stand in a ditch half full of water, I could feel my legs and feet going numb and then I couldn't feel anything at all.

The bloke who was with me said, "What do we do if we get one?"

"We take the bugger back."

"Did you hear that?" It was still pouring down.

"Yes I can hear it."

The Sergeant came round and said, "What are you lot doing with all this whispering?"

"What we're trained to do."

The enemy came past and started digging their trenches. So there we are in the pouring rain, us digging our trenches and them digging their trenches just a bit opposite us. We just sat there all night in the rain listening. I used to get the *Union Jack* newspaper and it always had a joke

The Nazi Party Long Service Award Medal given to Raymond Rush by a German soldier he was sent out to capture and take prisoner.
© Ian Sutton

in it. The joke should have been us and the Germans all digging facing each other and listening for each other, neither of us understanding a word.

On another patrol I did catch a prisoner. He thought he was going to die. I had no intentions of killing him because we needed him for interrogation. He begged me to take a medal in return for his life. Which I accepted and kept to this day.

The Allies to the north and south of 3rd Divisions A.O. were also pressing the Germans back in their own sectors, pushing them back to the wall that was the river Maas. Soon the whole area of the west bank of the Maas had been cleared of enemy positions and, along the line, men could catch their breath for a short while. Raymond and South Lancs reverted to the role of reserve battalion for 8th Brigade, leaving the 1st East Yorks and the 1st Suffolks as spearhead. In this formation, the Brigade occupied a compact area containing the villages of Geijsteren, Smakt and Maashees which put them on the west bank of the Maas. This area between Venray and the river was flat with little cover.

Raymond and the men were relieved when they received orders at the end of November to move to a rest area near Ghent, well away from the front line. Here to rest, reflect, reorganise and receive replacements of men and equipment. There were many holes in the roll call. Everyone had lost many friends. There were games and entertainment in the rest camps and even small parties were given leave to travel the short distance to Brussels for the culture, sophistication and night life.

Raymond Rush: They said, "Relax, we're stopping here for a bit." In the transit relief camp we got Tommy Trinder. He came over for entertainment. Arthur Askey sang that *Bee Song* that he was famous for. He used to dress up in skirts, never could understand why. One singer, Joan Piper, sang to us, I always thought about her, I can see her face. She never made it big though. Vera Lynn was in Burma at the time otherwise she might have come over to sing and we were told that she was due at any time. The next minute, the Germans had broken through and we shot out back to the front.

12th December saw the Brigade moving back to familiar territory on the west bank of the Maas. Raymond and the South Lancs were beginning to feel that it would be home from now on. They relieved 2nd Warwicks. From Vertrum to Vierlingsbeek they patrolled, clashing with elements of the German defenders from across the river who often crossed to make a nuisance of themselves. Things went on like this for a while and life quietened down until they received orders, on the 21st December, to move downstream to the Oostrum area to relieve the King's Own Scottish Borderers. Saturated ground from the relentless rains and flooding hampered operations. The men spent a miserable time digging into mud to make trenches that quickly filled with water. Everyone had wet feet. Clothing was saturated. Preparations were now advanced to effect a Rhine crossing and take the fight to the German homeland, however these preparations would have to wait. Hitler had a final throw of the dice and committed his last reserves in a desperate gamble. Success would strengthen his position for a negotiated truce, failure would open Germany to the Allies. The Battle of the Bulge, the Ardennes Offensive, would focus everyone's minds. The Rhine crossing would have to wait. Everything was at stake.

Raymond Rush: The Germans hit the American line hard and in no time at all it crumbled. As a consequence, we were scrambled to re-take the gap. There were American weapons left all over the place. It was there that I picked up an American assault rifle that held more rounds and was quicker to reload than the British one I was using, so I decided to keep it. Sometime later, the Sergeant Major pulled me up about it and confiscated it and used it for himself. I was a bit annoyed about that, as it was my trophy.

By the end of December 1944, the British and Canadians had a firm foothold in Holland. Belgium had been liberated. A short rest in Overloon where the men were served Christmas Dinner, well not exactly served. Raymond remembers.

Raymond Rush: We got to Overloon before Christmas Day. On Christmas Eve I was on duty on patrol on the front with a couple of the blokes. You could hear the German tanks or rockets moving through the night. You'd report that they were on the move and we would let fly at them. It was a dangerous position and I could see the water of the river glistening in the moonlight. If you saw a sudden movement in the dark it made you a nervous wreck.

"What was that? What was that?"

"Nothing there."

Christmas Day and we were in a big building where we cooked our own Christmas dinner. Outside was thick with snow. It was a really bad winter. My mate, John Reid, was a Lance Corporal and he said, "You don't have to go outside. There's plenty of fuel in here."

The only thing I regretted was we broke all the bloody furniture for the fire. We were in a big building. It could have been a church, I didn't really notice, I didn't really look at the architecture in them days. We were all very cold and very hungry.

"What're we having?"

"Let's have some of this pickled stuff."

"We shouldn't really trust it, it might be poison. Let's go for the livestock."

We all went out with our rifles to see what there was. Some of us had Tommy guns, and sometimes we were allowed a different weapon from our rifles. What bloody difference it made I don't know. So we all crept out watching for shadows and keeping out of the moonlight. Then we heard chickens.

"I'll get you, you bastard."

I was crawling round after this bloody hen. It'd stop and turn round and stare at me then it was off again. I just managed to get it by one of its legs. I had this revolver I got off this dead German and gave the hen a crack with it, so I thought I'd done my bit. It was bloody heavy too, an old broiler so I set to plucking it thinking, "Trust me to get an old hen."

Anyway Dan Baker was the cook, another Corporal he was. He says, "Alright lads, set the table, I'll do the cooking."

We had loads of cognac out of the barrel outside the shop. There was always a full barrel of cognac, you just went by and filled up. Only used to have Navy Rum at the time but I soon got used to the cognac. We had bottles of cider too. We got pissed as arseholes, all of us. I didn't know what I was doing. I heard the Sergeant shout, "Rushy lad, your rifle's on the ground."

"It can fucking stop there," I said.

We had set a long line of grates over the fire and just put all these hens on, feathers and all, they just got burnt off as the hens cooked. We sat there pissed. A chicken each like Kings.

"We'll never win the war like this," I thought.

We had a fiasco with all the food and booze. We could easily have been over run. Some of us were out cold. It was just coming dawn on Christmas morning, first light outside. "Stand to lads, stand to."

I was sitting on a chair. We didn't know where we were. We had knocked the window out and had the barrel of the Bren poking through it. It was all quiet but after a bit somebody shouted, "What was that?"

"Nobody there, shut up."

Tinkle, another tinkle, somebody was walking over our broken glass sound traps. "Some bugger's outside."

John Reid, a North East bloke shouted, "Right lads let 'em have it." And we opened up with everything we had, Mills bombs through the window, the Bren giving it to 'em. We threw everything at 'em, I had no ammo left in the end. Full light and everything went quiet again, even the Germans were quiet, no shells, nothing. Christmas Day and they starts singing *Silent Night, Holy Night*. So we started singing back then let fly with everything we had. Comical it was. We expected a counter-attack that never came.

We had white cloth wrapped round our rifles to camouflage it against the snow. We got ready for going across the river but we got called back. Then we heard the screams, somebody said, "It's one of our blokes."

It wasn't, it was a bloody big sow. We had pork for weeks after that, even the C.O. came round sniffing.

"That's a beautiful smell there lads, beautiful."

He was looking at it there, crackling and spitting on the grill. "Just lovely," he says watching the bloke turning it over and over.

He was proper aristocratic and he says, "Couldn't I just have a little bit?"

"No, fuck off."

You could call them anything, say anything to them, we still had discipline but we didn't give a shit. They were under fire the same as us. I came home from the war with more than a few swear words I didn't know before I went.

Raymond and the South Lancs spent most of Christmas 1944 on the front line. On New Year's Day night, they were attacked by a strong force of infantry. It was a short vicious exchange that caused casualties on both sides. The firing died down and the enemy withdrew.

Fighting patrols were sent out to advance to contact and assess the enemy strength that had hit them in the night but they found nothing. The Germans had gone and had removed their casualties in the darkness. A patrol came across an enemy position in a wood at the junction of the Beek stream and the main river. Raymond Rush and 'C' Company put in an attack, small arms and machine-guns barked in the darkness, tracer flew all around but they were beaten back. It was a bloody business. The attack failed and they were forced to withdraw.

Following a strategy of clearing the west bank of the Maas of any enemy, this enemy position had to be cleared. 'A' Company came up and tried again on 6th January. In support 'D' Company created a diversion at the edge of the wood and called on artillery for support. But, in spite of this, 'A' Company's assault failed when they came under accurate and sustained German artillery fire and were forced to withdraw. Raymond and 'C' Company relieved the battered 'A' Company and were tasked with keeping the wood under observation all that day and through the night.

The next morning, a squadron of armoured vehicles advanced through the wood and onto what was thought to be the enemy position that had been causing the South Lancs so much trouble, but they found that the Germans had evacuated during the night. Raymond remained in this area until January 15th when the arrival of 1st Suffolks as relief allowed the South Lancs to return to Brigade reserve at Venray.

Ray enjoyed ten days rest at Venray then it was back on the line. Because of the advances the Allies had made in the area, the 26th saw the South Lancs carrying out their first patrols on the far bank of the Maas. On the night of 29th/30th January successful patrols brought in two German prisoners and reams of useful intelligence.

A final desperate thrust by what remained of Hitler's reserves, in the Ardennes forest during the terrible winter of 44/45, had failed and been battered back. The "bloody bastards of Bastogne", the American 101st Airborne, had held out against overwhelming odds. The bruised and battered peoples of the occupation were at last liberated and were emerging from the rubble and destruction of what were once lovely towns and villages into the pale winter sunlight. Red-rimmed, tear and dust-stained eyes had seen almost five hard years of a German occupation that had brought terror, pain and a darkness that few believed would ever end. They were at last free and able to count the cost of the German army's cruel occupation. The Americans swept all in front of them in their race across France.

Raymond Rush: After Paris had been liberated there was a lull in the fighting. It was my turn to have twenty-four hours off. I was dropped off at a train station and given a ticket to Paris. I was to get off at a particularly station and go to a particular hotel. I was covered in mud and blood from the battles. I was looking lost. A French woman from the train approached me and asked where I was going. I explained I had to go to a particular hotel. She knew it well and said she would take me there. She grabbed my arm and takes me off to this hotel. She books me into the hotel. We go up to the room. She told me to strip. Someone came in and took my clothes away. She gave me a bath and kept me company all night. When I woke up, she's gone but all my clothes had been washed and pressed. I put them on and go downstairs and ask how much do I owe?

"Absolutely nothing at all."

That was my rest and recuperation. Then it was back to battle.

On 5th February 1945, Ray was with his battalion at a rest area at the little Belgian town of Werchter. Today the town hosts a major European rock festival but back in 1944 it was a small town swamped by Allied soldiers enjoying a brief interval from the war. It is roughly 40km from Antwerp. Raymond was a long way from the front for once. He stayed here for two weeks, training as usual but mostly enjoying some well-earned rest and entertainment with his pals. A lot of leisure and personal time was allowed in what were very pleasant surroundings. The men of the South Lancs long remembered the hospitality and the kindness of the people of Werchter.

The area of ground between the Maas and the Rhine, known as the Rhineland, had to be cleared of any lingering enemy troops before the Allies could attempt the Rhine crossing into Germany. The Canadian and British needed to consolidate on the west bank of the Rhine unopposed and free of interference before they could execute their plans to cross. While Raymond was at Werchter, the battle to claim this Rhineland had begun. A broad sweep of armour and mechanized infantry along this narrow strip was well underway and a forced crossing of the Rhine and a push into the German heartland was now a definite possibility.

Chapter Seven

OPERATION VERITABLE

An attack to the south east of Nijmegen by Canadians on 8th February, began the offensive. The 2nd British army was holding their positions on the Maas and, further south, the American 9th army was probing towards the Rhine looking desperately for a bridge that hadn't been blown by the enemy.

Raymond and the 3rd division were kept in reserve and out of the fighting until the third week in February. The offensive had successfully cleared the forested Rhineland and, at last, Raymond and 3rd division had reached the front. Now Operation Veritable could be put into practice. Raymond moved to the west bank of the Rhine to a town called Emmerial. Then he moved south east between the two rivers. Once in position, the initial phase was a frontal assault by the infantry with some armoured support. The defenders were well prepared and a hail of fire met the lead elements of the attack force.

Against stiff opposition they captured the ancient and strategic German town of Goch, which lay to the south east of Nijmegen, almost at the point where the two rivers meet and close to the border of the Netherlands. Bad weather had made life difficult even for men who were now used to fighting in bad weather. Goch was flattened by the fighting. The Germans had released the waters of the Roer and the Urft dams to cause a water surge that flooded the whole area. The German positions resembled small islands in the midst of the flooded woods. The flooded areas made movement, operations and patrolling difficult. Often the men had to wade through waist deep water. Life was grim but, in true South Lancs spirit, Raymond and the men carried on with grim and difficult tasks. In spite of the resistance, the terrain, the weather and the conditions, Operation Veritable was a great success. [1]

---

1. "There were often static battles until Operation Veritable, also known as the Battle of the Reichswald, started. It proved to be a decisive turning point towards the end of the Second World War. During Veritable, the Allies lost 23,000 men, the Germans 38,000." www.holland.com

Sketch by Raymond Rush

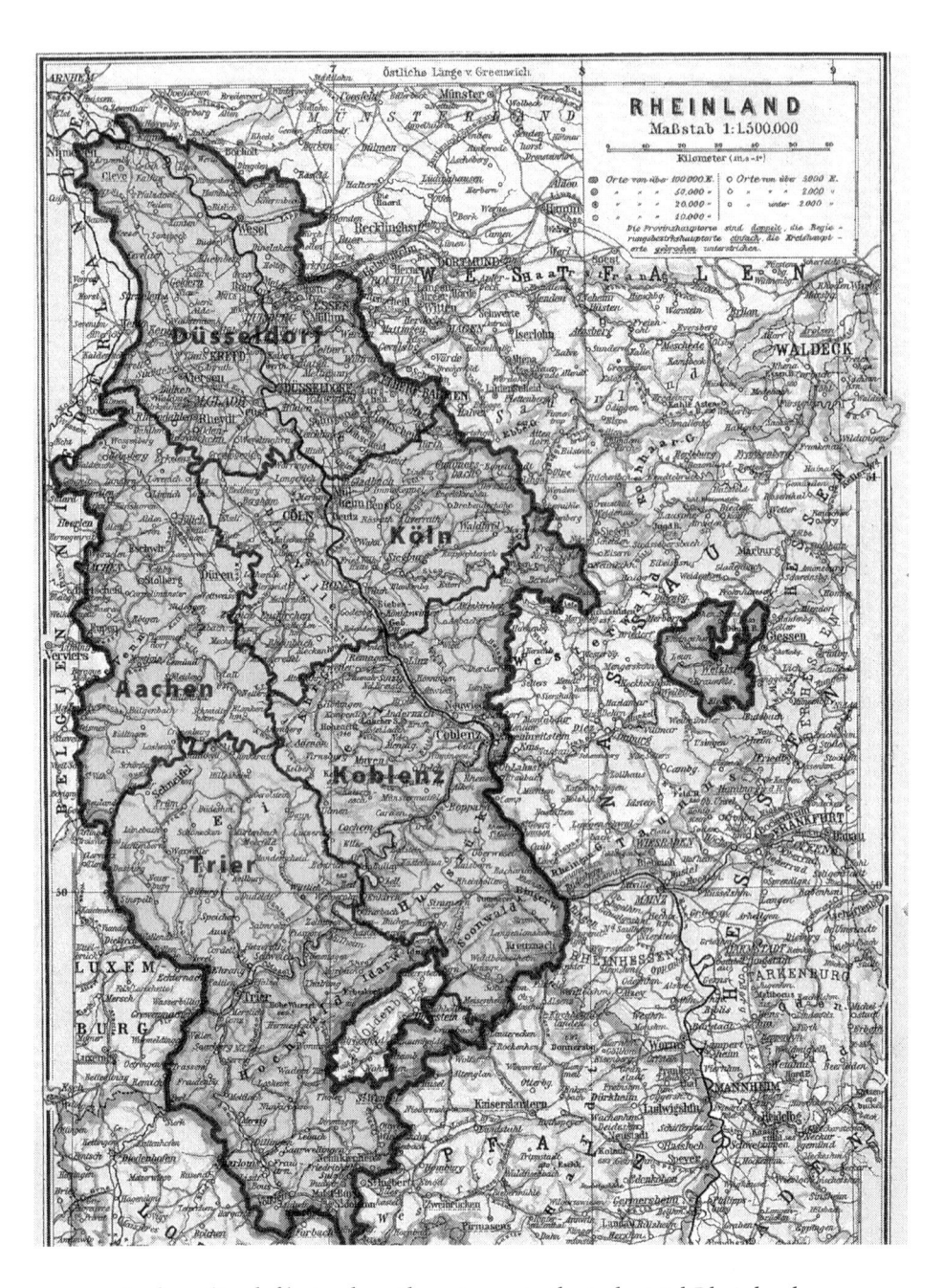

Arnhem (top left) stands as the gateway to the industrial Rheinland.

CODE-NAME: GRENADE

With the enemy mostly gone from the Rhine's left bank, the second phase, the Rhine crossing itself, could now be put into operation. Code-named "Grenade", it started on 23rd February. Raymond Rush and 3rd division relieved 15th Division and spent the night at Dutch the town of Tilburg. There they received orders to move back to the Goch area on the northern border of the German Rheinland.

They were in position by the 25th and spent a fairly quiet night. It rained heavily and no one could get dry. Occasionally they were shelled by the German gunners across the river but this was an expected part of life so close to the border.

A grey dawn brought an end to Raymond's quiet night. Early on the 26th, the Canadians had put in a massive attack on a strong enemy position east of Goch. The Germans there were hand-picked and experienced paratroopers. Raymond and the South Lancs found themselves caught up in this grimly fought battle. Very heavy fighting resulted in casualties on both sides. Ray barely had time to get his breath back when, early on 27th February, the South Lancs received orders to clear a wooded area to the south of the Canadians positions to the east of Goch. The German defenders put in a fierce and doggedly determined resistance and the South Lancs were hard pressed to achieve their objectives. The Suffolks took the lead and, experiencing much slighter resistance, made good progress.

South Lancs passed through them but were slowed by felled trees. The Germans by now were very skilled at preparing defensive positions in the dense forests. The middle of the wood hid German machine-gun nests and snipers which slowed the advance considerably. The rattle of machine-gun rounds and the buzz of sniper's rounds whizzing about their heads focused the men's thinking and forced them to go to ground until a flanking movement silenced some of the enemy's fire. In spite of this, the enemy would still prove persistent and wouldn't give up their positions without a fight. All attempts to force a way through the wood had failed. By nightfall, the South Lancs had begrudgingly admitted they could go no further against this stubborn defence and so were forced to consolidate their positions and go firm a few hundred yards from their objective. The day's fighting had been very costly. Five officers and twenty-five other ranks had been killed, two officers and forty other ranks had been wounded and four other ranks were missing believed killed in action. Thirty-four 3rd Infantry Division men would be left behind in the Dutch countryside.

British Churchill tanks and infantry en route to Reichswald, 8 February 1945.

The Rhineland, Udem, 24 February 1945
© Captain Edward K Deeming, 15th/19th King's Royal Hussars

Eventually the enemy's flanks were turned and so the South Lancs managed to reach, cross, and exploit the area beyond the wood and the main road that ran through it. After twenty-four hours rest, Raymond moved forward again to just south of Udem.

On the afternoon of 28th, he and the company moved forward to a concentration area, north of the railway that ran the length of the Waal. There they dug in again. The enemy had abandoned the bridgehead and left the area so, joined by the rest of the brigade, the planned forward move could go ahead. Further successes and the advances made by the Canadians meant that, by 11th March, the armies of the north were lined up along the west bank of the river Rhine from Neuss near Düsseldorf to Nijmegen and were looking into Germany at last.

All that remained was to coordinate a crossing of the river Rhine by the British and Canadians in the north and the Americans in the south, rush into Germany and finish the Third Reich off once and for all. The enemy had blown all the main bridges, so what was left was the unenviable task of forcing a crossing and establishing bridgeheads on the further bank that could be reinforced and strengthened.

The memory of Market Garden was still fresh in the Allies minds and almost everyone agreed that an opposed crossing by boat was not favoured. But luck favours the bold. When an American patrol found that the Ludendorff railway bridge at Remagen was still standing, the Americans knew they had found the Germans Achilles' heel. It was the only bridge left that crossed the Rhine. Why it was still intact has been debated by historians over the years. The popular belief is that a German General believed that it would be needed for either a counter-attack or a life-line for trapped and battered German divisions desperately trying to escape France and get home. It had been built to transport men, materials and supplies to the German front during the First World War and was named after a famous German general. But now it would hasten the fall of Nazi Germany. The movement of men and materials would soon flow in the opposite direction and in great numbers.

On the 7th March, the Americans captured the bridge and crossed it. Their armour poured over and began to fan out into Germany.

The Saarland, the forested German state bordered by France and Luxembourg, was quickly overrun. The major towns of Mainz and Worms were captured. The British and Canadians would soon join their American brothers on Nazi soil.

By the third week in March, the Allied armies were massed along the whole length of the Rhine, the dam had burst at Remagen. Thousands of German prisoners had been taken, the fight had been battered out of them and their armies severely depleted. Having few resources left, the Germans had left children and old men behind to defend the towns and villages. Naturally, they were no match for the battle-hardened Allies. The end of the Germans as an effective fighting force was near. Operations 'Varsity' and 'Plunder' were a combined action to put Canadian and British troops on the other side of the river with the ultimate aim of the destruction of Nazi Germany. Operations would be devised and executed to push the enemy back and keep them on the run and force his surrender.

The night of 23rd March saw the Allies launch the invasion that had been sought for so long. A massive airborne drop of 16,000 paratroopers and air-landing infantry from thousands of aircraft was coordinated with the actual crossing by the infantry at multiple crossing points.

A successful link up was effected. The resistance had been weaker than anticipated. The German formations were degrading in both numbers and quality and, taken by complete surprise, they were overrun. All Allied objectives were quickly secured. The German intelligence service here had been woeful. They really had no idea where the Allies had planned to drop and cross.

Raymond and the South Lancs took no part in the operation in its early stages. They remained in the Wesel area in Germany. It proved a quiet place to wait for further orders except for sporadic shelling by the desperate enemy. On the evening of 28th March 1945, orders came for the South Lancs to finally cross the wide fast-flowing river Rhine at Mülheimer in Mühlenfeld but without, of course, using the bridge. It had been destroyed by Allied bombing.

Raymond Rush: Me and this bloke were arrested by the MPs. We were out of our minds. "I'm not crossing any more water." I thought. When I heard that we would have to cross the Rhine in boats, my mind went back to the D-Day landings and what that was like and all the bridges I had crossed under fire.

The Sergeant Major got me in and interrogated me. Our O. C. Major Williams was there as well. We had crossed so many canals and bridges, the last time we were crossing this canal near Goch and we went over this little bridge in this jeep. The driver had his foot down but I was begging him to go faster. I thought, "Faster you bugger."

88 Shells were landing right by us in the water. We were getting soaked with the water splashes they were exploding that close. We got out of it.

Major Williams charged us. I can't remember what the charge was, and there was uproar outside the office.

I thought, "I'm going home. He's bound to be sending us home."

He said, "Will you accept my punishment?"

I said, "Yes, of course I will." What else could we do?

"Do you know where you're going?" he asked.

The other bloke says, "To Blighty, Sir."

"Are you bloody hell," he says. "There's our trucks. You two get in." He sounded stern so we gets in. "You two are going to Italy." That was that, no crossing for us, we were leaving the South Lancs.

There was no more fighting in Italy, the Germans and Italians were beaten. The only fighting was between Marshall Tito's Yugoslav communists and the Italians over land and we were to keep them apart as well as guarding POW's and displaced persons. I think I was sent to Italy because I was the only one left from the first wave on Sword beach, all my old mates were gone, everyone else were replacements. So I think he thought I'd done enough already and was giving me easier duties. I had been in the fighting for almost ten straight months; almost every week since June 6th. The next day the battalion went over the Rhine in rubber boats and the water was going faster and faster. A lot of them drowned.

We can't say for sure why Raymond's CO did not discipline him for what was clearly disobeying a direct order. The war had changed people, but the excellent officers that commanded the South Lancs knew their men. This was more of a reward than anything else. Raymond Rush was the last man standing and maybe his CO thought he had done enough, that he had crossed enough water and that his battalion and his country had asked enough of him. But it wasn't yet time for him to go home.

Raymond Rush (right) in Italy, 1948

Chapter Eight

ITALY - PRISONERS OF WAR AND DISPLACED PERSONS

The war across Europe with its horrors, of murder, ethnic cleansing, genocide and the destruction of whole cultures, had uprooted millions of people. They had been driven from their homes across the continent and had nowhere to go. Italy seemed one of the safest bets until the Germans were finally defeated but that was still a few months away. The majority were from Concentration camps, labour camps and POW camps that were being discovered as the Allies in the east and west rolled the Germans back. Over eleven million people were displaced, seven million alone from German concentration camps and POW camps. They came malnourished, ill, and dying. The Allies were doing their best to provide shelter, in many instances in old disused military barracks. As the war ended, these people had no homes left and nowhere to go. They needed to be resettled. The Allies sought to provide basic shelter, nutrition and health care. The psychological wounds inflicted on these people was immense, untrusting of authority and apprehensive of everyone, it added to the difficult tasks that befell soldiers like Raymond.

Not much has been written or recorded about the work done to resettle displaced persons or prisoners of war. They have become a forgotten multitude of millions who, by some miracle, made their way across Europe, into Italy and on to a new life. For the most part, we only have the actual accounts of men like Raymond Rush who carried out this heartbreaking work.

From early 1945 until his release and de mob from the army, Raymond carried out several duties in Italy. He mainly travelled up and down the East coast, accompanying trains full of displaced persons. Along with guard duties at the various camps he was kept busy. More dangerous duties found him trying to keep the peace between the Italians and Yugoslavs who were intent on capturing as much territory from each other as they could. It was a time of a post-war shake-up and old rivalries were beginning to surface.

Raymond Rush: I did nearly three years in Italy. This Civil War was raging between the Yugoslavs, in the hills that bordered Italy, and the Italians. I was out of the South Lancs and in another unit but I always wore my South Lancs and Divisional badges. We got to a place right on the coast. Every night you couldn't move for crowds parading for either Tito or the Italians. It was hot and sunny and, apart from these parades, it was quiet . And this was punishment?

I got sent to Pula in what is now Croatia but then it was Yugoslavia. Pula is on the Adriatic coast opposite Venice. Going over on the boat we were serenaded by this famous Italian opera singer, lovely voice he had. They told us there was a big parade on with all these Italians singing and the other lot chanting: "Tito! Tito! Tito!"

Next we were sent to Bologna in Italy. I can remember seeing this sign on the road in, 'Bologna'. Displaced persons and German POW's were placed in massive camps, all together. My job was to guard them. The administration to process all these people, and send them on their way to where they wanted to go, was tremendous. They could select which country they wanted to be sent to - Canada, America, Australia, lots of places. Where they had come from had been destroyed and I always thought they should be able to go back to where they came from, back to their homes. Most of the ones I guarded came from Germany. Our admin sorted them all out.

SS soldiers and officers were there and they were bastards. They made it much harder for us all the time. But it was beautiful, hot, gorgeous weather. We had left behind the hardest winter for decades in Germany. And now we were in sunshine. Our camp where we lived was in the POW camp and we were guarding the POW's who were in there. I used to write home and give my mum my address but I had to say that I wasn't in a POW camp myself, I was just guarding them. We had a good camp apart from these SS. We mounted a walking guard. We would walk miles all round the perimeter and pass each other, walking all night.

"All well."

"All well."

The SS were buggers always trying something. We had all their guns and ammo, all the stuff we'd captured, so they could have broken out at any time and stolen them. We took this little car and filled it with petrol, we used to use it for changing the guard instead of all the walking we had to do, but, one night, it broke down and it made us late. The officers thought we had gone missing. The Sergeant Major came looking for us, wondering where we were. He doubled us all the way back to the camp. So that was the end of the car.

It got very cold at night and you could feel the dew like rain falling, dropping on us. We got soaking wet with it. One night, we heard a noise outside. "That's a bloody horse that is."

"Course it isn't a bloody horse, horses neigh, that's not a neigh."

"It's a donkey."

So we captured this donkey, tried to make it go but it was having none of it, bloody stubborn it was. After a while, it got to know us better so we kept it and looked after it. We would change the guard with this donkey. It was all going so well until we got found out then that was the end of that.

In Italy there was a kid begging for cigarettes. I said, "Go on, bugger off." He went and fetched this German. He had his rifle and the German said, "Give him a cigarette or I'll shoot you."

I thought, "O aye," and bent down, Two Mills bombs dropped out of my ammo pouch.

"Oh, look what I've found," I said to him.

He soon buggered off. The Germans in Italy weren't very good troops. They were new conscripts, not like the ones we had been fighting.

I still have a pass, I don't know why I keep it. It's a pass that used to get me all the way down the Italian east coast on the train to Barletta from Verona. Me and another bloke got the job of escorting these trains that were bringing people back. We took them down to Barletta and were allowed to make our own way back, all up the coast. That was a good job. The train used to empty at Barletta and people we were transporting went into a transit camp. There were displaced persons, deserters mostly who daren't go back to where they came from, all different people, all different religions. We handed them over and from Barletta they shipped off to different countries. They had lost everything and I felt sorry for them. Compared to them I had a cushy life, but they didn't have to go down a street and have a bomb go off or a sniper shooting at them. You get used to the bullet going past you. There were those that wanted to carry on fighting for their own reasons even though the war was over. Doing that job we got to know the population.

I was in a little seaside town called Riccione, a beautiful coastal town, we were stuck there for weeks and weeks with all these displaced persons on the train. What they were eating I don't know but they managed to find enough food from somewhere. We couldn't do anything. There was only the two of us until the red caps came and gave us a hand. We had enough rations for ourselves for a fortnight. We always had a Lance Corporal with us but that made no difference, he was never the boss and we took no notice of him. We did what we wanted and he could please himself. Tins of sausages, tins of bacon, beautiful. We would go to the café in the town. There was this Italian American bloke outside who spoke English. He asked us if we wanted a Cathouse?

"Cathouse? What's a Cathouse?"

Somebody said, "It's a brothel. He's asking if we want a brothel."

"Clean," he said it was. "No diseases at all, no VD."

He could tell you everything about the girls.

I says, "If I catch anything I'll knock the shit out of you."

So we flog the rations to him for a tremendous price, it was like they were gold, and it's off to this Cathouse of his.

I sat in this bar having a meal, gorgeous meal it was, like a 5-Star hotel kind of meal. It was in a place called Lido di Jesolo just outside Venice. The bar was run by the Naafi but all the staff were Italian. The smell of the food was amazing. So this one night I was on my own waiting for my mate and this girl sat down at my table and she said in perfect scouse "Where are you from?"

"You won't know it," I said, "It's a little town called Prescot.

"Oh my God!" she says.

"Hang on," I says, "I know you, don't I?"

"You should do," she says, "I sat next to you in school."

"I do remember you now," I said, and we got talking and reminiscing. They were a big family and lived in a flat down by the police station.

"You've changed, you look really pretty, I must look haggard." I was putting the charm on.

"Oh you don't," she said.

I thought, should I chat her up, should I risk it? I didn't know how long I would be stationed here and I was a good Catholic. I went to church at least once a year. She takes me home with her and we got quite lovable. They had deported her and her family when war broke out as they were classed as undesirable aliens. They had a relative, Enrico Gilly, who was an Italian pop singer, he was the greatest tenor on earth. What a voice! That was near Venice early 1945.

We captured an SS General in Italy, Von something or other. We used to make the bastard sit in a barrel of cold water. That knocked some of the arrogance out of him. Saw it in a paper not long since that he had died. Somebody said he took his own life.

We were in Verona. We thought where can you go in Verona? There's only one place. San Marino, it's a small town in its own independent province. It was neutral during the war and was left alone. Full of communists. It's got a big racing track now. We spent a week there, no ladies unfortunately. The camp was in Riccione and San Marino was inland to the west. It was at the top of a mountain and had a wall all round it like Hadrian's Wall. I was into the ancient Roman stuff so I couldn't wait to go up there and see it. I went with my mate, Ivor. He gave me a top secret letter once that he wanted me to take back to England when I went back and only open it then. He said it was written in Italian and it was for his wife. I did take it back but I forgot about it and only remembered it seventy years later when I was sorting some stuff. So I opened it and because it was in Italian I got it translated. The bugger had had me on for seventy years because this so called top secret letter was a load of bullshit. It said rubbish like "I had a lovely meal" and nonsense like that. He did it to wind me up and it bloody worked! the bugger. I all along thought it was a secret letter that had important stuff in it. He died young, aged fifty-five which was no age really. When we got up to San Marino I had my photo taken in front of this wall.

I had boils all over my back and neck and a huge carbuncle under one arm so I went sick and told the M.O. that I couldn't do guard duty. He still sent me out on guard. Eventually, under persuasion, he signed me off. The cook's mate was a displaced German who was always hanging around. We made a deal me and him. He would get my boils sorted and I would help him to get out and get him on his way.

It turned out he was an SS medic and he said, "Hang on a minute, come inside," so I followed him. The next thing he had, as quick as a flash, cut all the tops of my boils off with scissors.

I shouted at him, "I'll effing kill you."

He shot off terrified and I chased him. Some SS men escaped that night. The next morning I told the CO what he had done and what had happened. "The German bastard," the CO said, "He can't do that to one of my men."

"I'll effing kill him," I said.

"Calm down Rushy, calm down," the CO said.

You could hear his SS mates shouting, "He's here, he's here."

"Come here you." He was terrified, I had my Tommy gun and I was going to bloody shoot him when I caught him. I chased him all round the camp and his SS mates were all cheering him on. He got winded and stopped running and was panting for his breath, I went up to him.

"Kamerad," he said

"Bugger off," I said. But the boils did get better, so it was 'thanks very much' in the end and I gave him some cigarettes. But he really did shit himself when he thought I was going to shoot him.

We had power cuts and stuff would get chucked over the fence in the darkness. The black market was rife. It went on every night, the chucking stuff over the fence.

Towards the end of my time, I had the job of escorting Jewish people down the length of Italy to the docks so that they could catch the ships that would return them to their homelands. It was the time when no one would have them, so they were all returning from all over Europe trying to get back to Israel.

Finally I got sent home, three years after D-Day. My overseas service was done, but I had to get to Cardiff before I could be de-mobbed proper. Some blokes took stuff home with them, things that they had found. I was in the line to clear customs to get back into the UK and, when I looked round, this bloke had a mangle strapped to his back. When questioned by the military police, he said he had promised his mam a mangle.

In the end it took me six weeks to get from Italy to Cardiff. So I gets there with all my kit, battle dress, kit bag, gas mask, everything and I bangs on the big doors to the barracks. The commander of the guard presented arms to me. He must have thought I was a Colonel. Proper cocky he was. I had a D.A. haircut[1] and lovely blonde hair. He looks at me and says, "Go straight down there, turn left, straight to the barber's shop and stand at ease until I get there." I slipped the barber a shilling to just give me a trim.

"No effing chance," he said. "Do you want me to lose my job?" He shaved me bald. A few weeks later on when I got to my mates in Birmingham he saw me and doubled up laughing and said, "Look at the state of his head. Look at that effing haircut!"

The RSM was on the square, massive square it was, and he says, "You're on parade in the morning."

I said, "No, I'm not, I'm finished."

So he says, "You're not effing finished yet, you're on parade."

After everything I had done and all the places I had been, I was still in the army so I didn't have a choice. I thought, "Here we go, another bloody parade." He marched us all around the town.

I went to Blackpool straight from the camp at Brecon where I met a hal-Welsh half-English man. We joined in with some Scottish regiment

---

1. Acronym for Duck's arse. A popular hair style for young men at that time with a long hair combed back around the sides, and parted centrally down the back of the head.

who were there drinking. I eventually got home weeks later. I'd had three months leave and there was nothing to go home for. So I got the train to Liverpool and went to the ticket collector. "Sorry lad," he says, "You're on the wrong train."

I couldn't argue so I got my head down and started to walk home. This bloke pulls up in a black cab. "Where are you going?" he says.

I said, "Prescot."

He took me straight to my front door for free. This was nice because the pictures would let you in to see a film for free and shops would give you things for free but this was a nice surprise. The door opens and Aunty Alice, mum's sister, grabs me.

"Hey Jessie, he's home. Your lad's home."

Mother's stood by the fire. I hadn't been home for four or five years. I never had any wages until I got to Germany, so I was due a fortune with all my overseas pay due. I sent money home to my mother and, when I got home, I found out that she'd saved every penny of it to give back to me. She'd saved the bloody lot. Mother said, "So you've come home have you?"

He was home then, my dad, and I wanted him out, I tried everything to get him to fight me. I once slung all his clothes out onto the front lawn. I tried all sorts.

I went to get my demob suit, I came to this big warehouse and got this cracking suit, herringbone tweed and a waistcoat. I managed to wear the waistcoat out in the 1960's, over ten years it lasted. I was really shy when I was younger in the army, the MO started to help me get over it. He said I should start by whispering, "I do not blush, I do not blush," over and over again, then make it gradually louder and louder, "I do not blush, I do not blush." Keep going until I was shouting it, "I do not blush, I do not blush." It didn't cure me. I was nineteen or twenty and I couldn't go into a pub without blushing.

ARMY BOOK X 801

Surname ...... *Rush*
Initials ...... *R.*
Army No. *14664420*

SOLDIER'S RELEASE BOOK

CLASS "A"

> Any person finding this Book is requested to hand it in to any Barracks, Post Office, or Police Station, for transmission to the Under Secretary of State, The War Office, London, S.W.1.

> This book must be presented at the Post Office whenever you cash a postal draft or one of the drafts in your payment book, to enable the Post Office official to record the date of payment on the inside page of the front cover.

51-5235

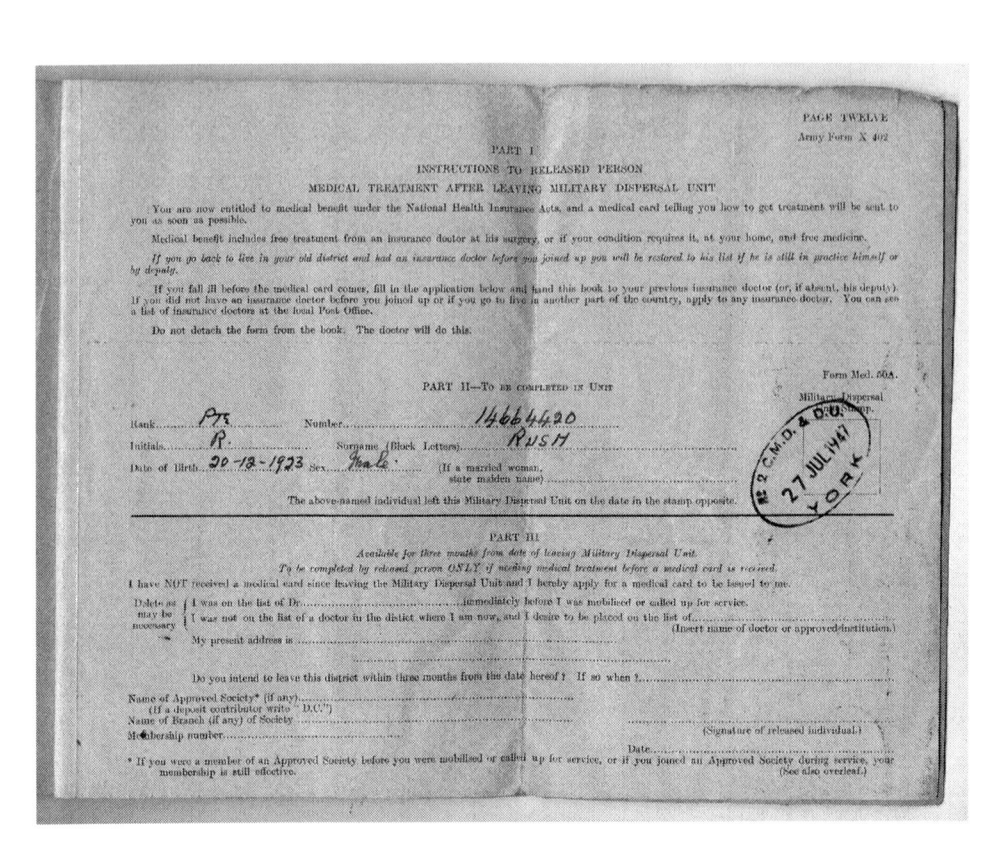

Pages from Raymond Rush's Release Book

'Military Conduct - Good. Works well without supervision. A clean, sober, well turned out man. Intelligent and dependable."

POST OFFICE STAMP SHOWING DATE OF PAYMENT

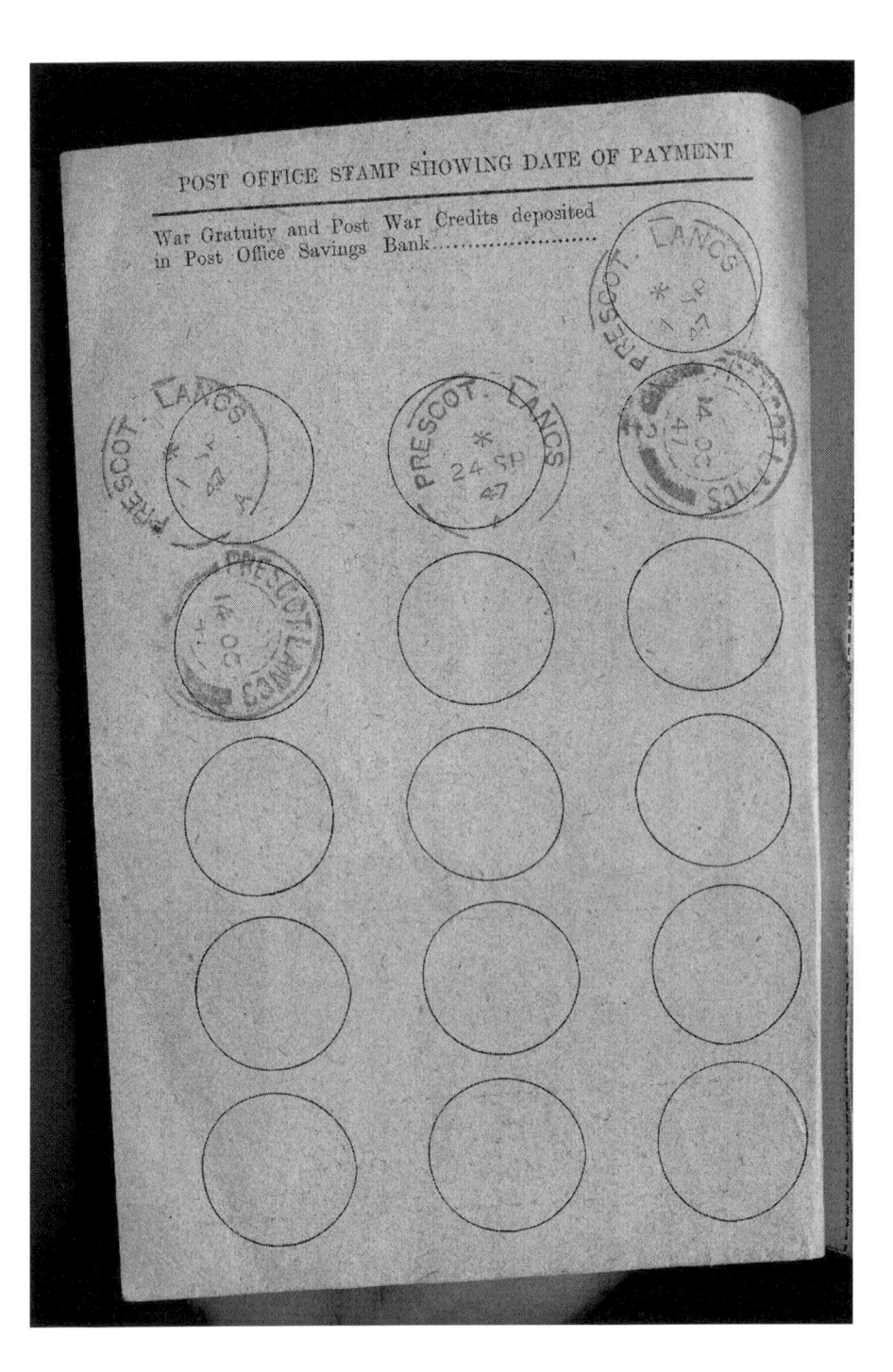

War Gratuity and Post War Credits deposited
in Post Office Savings Bank..........................

ON HIS MAJESTY'S SERVICE

PAGE ONE (A)

NO STAMP REQUIRED.

Postage Prepaid by War Office.

The Officer i/c .... Records,
SOUTH WALES BORDERERS.

at .... Preston

.... Lancs

Initials......... R. .... Surname (Block Letters) 14664420
Date of Birth...20-12-1923... Sex......Male......... RUSH
(If a married woman, state maiden name).........

The above-named individual left this Military Dispersal Unit on the date in

PART III

Army No....14664420.... Present Rank........PTE.........
Unit........Rytt Depot
Regiment or Corps....SOUTH WALES BORDERERS.
Surname (Block Letters)......... RUSH
Christian Name/s (in full)......... Raymond.
The receipt of this man's greatcoat is hereby acknowledged.
Signature of O.C. Civilian Clothing Depot.........
Place.........
Date......... 183028

Note.—In cases where a soldier is not in possession of a greatcoat, the certificate on the reverse of this form should be completed.

Chapter Nine

AFTER THE WAR

After the war, I started courting my wife. My sister-in-law was a housekeeper to a Sergeant Major. I regretted serving my apprenticeship as a joiner for just four years because, when I came home from the war, I was nearly twenty-four-years old and I could not get a job at my trade. They always asked me for my Union Card but I didn't have one. They never thanked me for my war service, or took it into account. They never called us 'Heroes'. They just rejected me because I wasn't in the Union.

I started keeping pigs and fowl in Rainford, the land was owned by the Nevins family and I rented some off Jack Nevin. I had fourteen pigs in all. He was an ex-army officer and used to ride out on his white horse on a Sunday morning and I used to race him back to St Helens, him on his horse and me running, I knew the quick ways the horse couldn't go so I won. He expected bowing and scraping from me but I would never do that. Bacon was rationed and all us farmers used to take it in turns to slaughter a pig to sell. One night it was pouring down and the dog was barking, I get to the pig shed and can hear whisperings, so I picked up some dropped turnips and start throwing them into the piggery to chase them off. They were after stealing my pigs.

I was travelling from Sutton Road, where our house was, to the piggery at Rainford. My wife said it was a long way to go to work, so she comes home one night and says, "I've got a present for you." It was a tandem bike, a cracking bike it was and had brakes and everything. She paid £6 for it. So I went to work on a tandem bike. We used to go for rides on it with my wife in front and me behind and anyone who knows about riding a tandem knows it's hardest at the back, she wasn't daft.

I looked after the pigs for twelve months then thought I should get a cleaner job. I went everywhere looking for a job, even Whiston hospital. I was in my uniform with my medals and I saw the matron. She said, "You won't like it here, you won't like the blood, you're not the type."

I looked at her and thought, "I've not long since come home from war."

I went up the road to Whiston fire station to join the fire service, again I was in uniform. This bloke came out, his belly out here and he had his defence medal from the first war pinned to his tunic.

"How old are you?" he said, "You've got to be fit to do this job. See that tower over there?"

It's still there to this day.

"The top of the tower with you, run up and down that ladder."

"I'll do it if you want me to," I says, "But if I do it you have to do it as well.

"I can't do that," he said, "I'm station master. What chest measurement are you?"

"I'm 38 ½ inches," I said.

"What weight?"

"112 lb."

He said, "'re you sure?"

I said, "I'm positive, I've just had an examination coming out of the army."

"That's eight stone," he said.

"You're a good reckoner," I said.

He said, "Hang on a minute." He went back in the room, "I'm sorry you're not big enough."

"What do you want? A 5ft 4" gorilla?"

"You're being sarcastic."

"I'm not being sarcastic."

I was Mr. Angry in them days, "You can stuff your fire brigade." I was a real nowty bugger then. After all that walking round I went to Widnes on my bike. I tried the cement works and got a job there and got paid extra for working with cement.

"When do you want me to start?" I asked.

"Night turn tonight," he said.

I got talking to a mate at Prescot pool hall and he asked me where I was working? I told him Sidac in Widnes. He said it's a killer working with cement. Nobody had told me that so I went straight back to work and went upstairs into the office.

"Get me cards ready," I said

"You can't do that, we need a weeks' notice."

I told him that I hadn't yet worked a week so I didn't have to give notice.

"Get me cards straight away."

"Why are you leaving?" he asks.

"I want to smell fresh air."

I was still on army pension and three month's pay with 6d a day for overseas service. I goes to Sutton rolling mill, "Any jobs going here? I'll brush up if you want?"

He gave me an application form and told me to bring it back on Monday. I went back with it. "You want a job? No problem, sit down there." He was a charge-hand on good money, they paid the best round here. I got a job on the lithographic. We were rolling lithographic zinc sheets for color printing papers. I was there a couple of years. I got married. We were saving up when I got my wage-packet one Friday, there was two weeks' pay plus a bonus and a redundancy notice. 'No longer required,' it said, 'Will send for you if work picks up.'

So I was walking down the East Lancs road looking for jobs when this van pulls up, a Greenall's brewery van it was.

"Where are you going?" he asks.

We had a mortgage and my wife was working but I still really needed a job.

"I'm looking for work but it's all fields round here."

He said he would drop me off in Kirkby and pick me up on my way back. I asked in every factory there was. Nothing doing. I started back home up the East Lancs, stepping out to get to Windle Island where I turn off for home. He pulls up. "I can't take you beyond Windle in case somebody sees me with a passenger, I'd be in trouble. I only live at the back of you, I'll get in touch if I hear of anything at our place."

I got a letter through the letter box.

"Be at Greenall's in Hall Street, St. Helens, on Monday."

He didn't even know me name. I went. The bloke was all posh with a collar and tie. "Come in," he says.

He saw me and came to attention.

"No need for that," I said, "My serving's done."

"Can you read and write in pencil?"

"Oh yes, I can join 'em up as well.

He said, "That's alright, start next Monday, 8 till 5."

They gave me a book, pen and pencil, I had to write the number of barrels of beer going out in my book and where they were going. This could be my way up to the top, I was telling my wife. At the time I had no idea about maths or physics. I came out of school reading and writing with basic arithmetic. I got £6 1 shilling and a penny for a week's wage. They took 5 shillings for national insurance and our mortgage was £4, 15 shillings. We were laughing. My wife got the manageress job at the Co-op and the mother-in-law looked after our baby, so he got fed proper. It was great. I stayed there until I retired many years later.

Actually, I took retirement because Mr. Greenall closed the brewery in 1975 after losing patience with the union who kept making ridiculous demands. The final straw came when the delivery drivers demanded he buy them all better sunglasses and biros. They went out on strike when he told them to buy them themselves. So he closed the factory. Greenall's had been employing thousands in St. Helens since 1762.

I love where I'm living now at Colliers Croft, a nursing home in Haydock. It's the best place I've ever lived. Old people should be living like Lords because of what we did. Everyone should have the same quality of care when we get old. I'm a World War Two veteran and I've had to sell my house to pay for my care here. It's not right. It makes you feel that everything you've earned and owned doesn't belong to you, it belongs to somebody else. It's not right that the state doesn't pay for your care when you get older. You end up with all this money you've saved and they take it all off you in your old age.

I find my happiness instead my friends and I've got plenty of them. Ethel was a friend of my wife's and I got a card from her only the other day. They met and became friends in Prescot and we've remained friends after my wife died. We sent letters to each other and kept in touch. She married Alfred who was a pork butcher and we used to get our pies and sausages from him. When I had the piggery we were saving up for a deposit on a house. They were planning to build some bungalows on some lovely land in Rainhill. When we went walking there, I used to think it would be nice to build a bungalow on some of that land. So I went one morning and pegged a space out but had no chance of raising the deposit in time. Vi was expecting and had a manager's job at the Co-op. Doctor Bates was a very important man in the town, everybody knew him. He had been the Lord Mayor many times over. His wife was a great friend of my mother-in-law. They used to make clothes, wedding and bridesmaid dresses and children's clothes. When Vi was expecting I took her to see Mrs Bates when she invited us for tea one Monday night. We had a nice meal served by her servants. Doctor and Mrs Bates were top notch people, and they had a son who was a heart specialist. We were having coffee with her one day and she had her servants give me a few brandies. I thought, "What a life."

She said to us, "I could help you, you know."

My ears pricked up.

"I could lend you some money," she said. "I've got lots."

I looked at Vi, I was up for it but I wasn't sure of Vi.

"Oh, we couldn't think of it," I said, "We should go to the building society."

"Better you take my money," she said.

We were at a function and she came across to us and showed us some pictures of wedding dresses that she had made. She said to Vi, "I've put a cheque in the post for you."

"How much is it?" asks Vi.

"£600," she says.

That's a lifetime's wages back then, a small fortune. Back then you could build a house from the foundations up for £1,800.

I said, "If we take this money, Mrs. Bates, we'll be forever in your debt."

I didn't mind that and I looks at Vi. Vi said, "I'm okay with it."

Mrs. Bates was just a lovely, kind lady. Her husband was always off attending functions so she was on her own quite a bit. She used to sit in with him when he held his surgeries and she went out on patients' house calls with him in their bloody big car with its chauffeur. So we took the money off her.

When I got older and a bit more prosperous, and I had the money to pay her back, she would never take it off me. She used to say it was a present. At that time I always used to worry about being made redundant and paying the mortgage and she came to the rescue at just the right time, just when we needed it. It's nice to be helped when nobody else has helped us. It's been a good life for me really in one sense.

Lancashire-sur-Mer in Normandy—Hermanville

By CAPTAIN HUGH GUNNING

[Former Manchester journalist, who landed with the Third British Infantry Division on D-Day.]

Hermanville, Wednesday.

ON the eve of "Le Jour de Debarquement" I came back to make a tour of this memorable beachhead in Normandy. "The Day of Disembarkation" is the French name for the anniversary of D-Day, an event which is now, after only two years, firmly established in the French calendar. The French make it an occasion for doing tribute to the men who fell in the assault on the beaches.

And the men they acclaimed were assault troops of the 1st Battalion the South Lancashire Regiment, specially chosen with the 2nd East Yorkshires for the attack on Queen Beach, the most-easterly landing place in the invasion operation.

When the South Lancs went ashore they, and the East Yorks, were the only seaborne troops on the left flank of the long coastline attack. The only other British soldiers in that corner of Calvados were the men of the Airborne Division, who had seized intact the previous night the vital bridge over the Canal du Caen at Benouville.

The South Lancs had their first casualties on Queen Beach,

SHOCK OF BATTLE

The Commanding Officer of the South Lancs was killed and they had other losses, but they won their beach, and, turning right, they entered Hermanville, whose people were still dazed by the shock of battle.

Here in Hermanville these men from the North had their first brief pause in the battle, and they did a typical Lancashire thing. They made tea—the first recorded brew-up in our Third Divisional beach-head. The hour was 10 a.m.

Hermanville has not forgotten her first liberators from Lancashire.

For future pilgrims from Lancashire there is another place in Hermanville to which they will turn their steps, the beach cemetery, a sheltered tree-lined field which is already bright with the flowers of June, the homage of these good Norman villagers.

Lieut.-Colonel R. P. H. Burbury, who was killed on the beach, is buried here between two soldiers

his right, and Private Rogerson, T., 3783312, on his left.

The men and machines have gone from the beach-head, have vanished like a mirage, leaving only the rows of white crosses and the shattered villages set in a golden land of buttercups. Nature in Normandy is winning back her own—indeed has won it back already, for the battlefields of 1944 are raising the harvest of 1946.

Queen Beach was the South Lancs Beach on Sword.

Here is the monument built by the French as a tribute to the D-Day assault troops. It is on a road which formed one of the main exits from Queen Beach—most easterly landing-point in the invasion, and on which the South Lancashires landed.

My Mother sent me this cutting from the daily paper, weeks after we landed. I think she must have been proud, although she had already lost one son.

Pasted into his diary is the 'tea brew' newspaper cutting

Chapter Ten

RAYMOND RUSH'S DIARY 2011-2012 (extracts)

This is Friday morning now. I am getting ready to go to my cousin Pat's for our ritual hotpot and good conversation. I am not a good talker. Of course it boils down to education which I never got. I am a good listener and my head is bursting with things I've seen and heard and now it is the time to get it off my chest.

October 10th, 2011. A dedication service at the parish church in Prescot, at two o'clock, for all those men and boys who worked for the BICC and lost their lives for H. M. Service.[1] Went to my brother's son, Malcolm, today (9th) to let him know his Dad's name will be on a new plaque. The old one was lost when they knocked the factory down (I should have said when they killed Prescot). The plaque was made of recycled machinery taken from the factory. The service was conducted by the Bishop of Warrington. All the usual dignitaries were there from Knowsley Council. A very moving service for relatives and friends of the comrades on the Cenotaph. As it is, it is just a few yards from my grandmother's grave, and where my mum's ashes are.

Well it's that time of year that I have come to not like. Five years ago, I spent Christmas Day in hospital with Vi. She took ill just about dinner time. It was touch and go then but she came to. I was hoping she would live a bit longer to see her first great grandchild, Alfie. She hung on till Christmas was over and, in January, she died in her sleep.

I have never had nightmares since I got married but I did have them when I was living at my mum's. That's when I had a job as a herdsman at the pig farm. But I had one last nightmare the last time I was in hospital this year. I woke up during one night, or so I thought, but obviously I was asleep. I saw shadows walking about with helmets on. The first thing

---

1. Seventy three were killed in service during the Second World War. The factory was demolished in 1991. The original plaque (and one for the First World War) were moved to the Pirelli plant in Carr Lane, where they stood until 2007. The memorials are now in the grounds of St Mary's parish church.

I knew I started shouting out, "Hey, what's going on! You can't do that to him," (that's the fellow in the next bed). The next thing I woke up with a nurse saying, "Come on love, it's only a nightmare." They were treating the man in the next bed. He was having something changed. The nurse brought me a cup of tea and said, "Drink this and go to sleep. You can dream of me, no problem." It's funny but I still have to sleep with a light on at night. Writing this book is like talking to someone. I am alone and have been alone at times all my life. I miss my two comrades from the army, my true friends for life, and there's just me left to tell all our tales but no one wants to listen. Anyway, they would not believe a word you said. If only they knew what we went through. There's only me left. And so I will have my Horlicks and watch a crap film about how the Americans won the war.

Does Raymond carry any scars? Yes of course he does. 75 years on and Raymond and men like him still suffer as a result of their wartime experiences. The only help and support they got on demobilization and return to normal life was in many cases to be advised to "Chin up, best foot forward, and to carry on." He still has a short pamphlet he was given that refers him to certain obscure publications on mental health and dealing with stress.

Raymond Rush: The world and the people are changing and I don't like it. I always think of that old Henry Hall song before the WWII it was, *Money is the root of all evil*. And it's getting worse. God help the next generation. No-one thinks of anyone else but themselves. My generation looked after each other in bad times, which I can say was worse off than these days. You must bear in mind that I am writing these thoughts when I get lonely. If I had someone here with me, they would be getting an ear bashing. Still, I can always start an argument with myself in my beloved No.7. I thought I would spend a minute putting them down instead of bottling them up. They say the pen is mightier than the sword, and I believe it.

Raymond was still playing golf when he was ninety-three.

It is not as strenuous as when I was young because my friends, all wrinklies, now have buggies between us, and we only play for fun and exercise. We are all pretty fit, that means we can walk if we have to. I have stopped walking to the club at night after a disturbing night trying to get past a gang of yobs. One or two would not have bothered me, but more than that you don't argue, do you?

I hadn't been well, so going to the club on New Year's Eve was out. I hadn't been dressed for nearly a week so what should I do? I didn't even have a brandy in the house to let the New Year in, so I got the little box with the piece of coal in and a sugar lump, which Violet used to put in my pocket. I put it in my dressing gown pocket, filled a glass with a treble whisky, put the kettle on and waited for the bells and fireworks to start. I wrapped myself up well and went out the back door and dashed in the front. I will never get used to all that noise, fireworks and bangs. I put some of the hot water in my glass for a hot toddy. It doesn't cure anything but it lets you forget. I felt a lot warmer after that. So off to bed with my treble whisky after wishing myself, "Ray, a very happy New Year", and I thought I heard Vi whisper, "I love you too." I don't remember anything else till morning but my glass was empty.

Went to St. Helens Museum on Sunday. [2] Spent a good morning there. The place was packed. What a massive place it is. I never knew it existed before. I went right back in time. Then I had my dinner in Lily's Victorian tea place in Hall Street. What a beautiful place she has. Pat has started making rice pudding for after dinner on Fridays, not tinned but like our mum used to make, and she always gives me the dish to scrape. We used to fight for it when we were all at home in the old house in Market Place. Our hotpot club is growing bigger every week. Cousin Janet came on Friday. It sounded like a madhouse, everyone talking and laughing, but I love it. To think I started it all by having a hotpot from the market. But Pat started making her own which is much nicer. And word spread. It's nice to see your relatives pretty often. It keeps you in touch, with no secrets. I like David a lot. Nothing is too much trouble for him. All my mother's side of the family are great. I love them all.

---

2. The World of Glass, on the banks of England's first canal.

I'm reading Vera Lynn's autobiography, what a woman! I saw her before we went overseas. We were all in love with her. I am a good-time traveller, only going back. I don't want to see the future any more, only the present and the past, and the past is my favorite time. I remember all the good things but the bad things still haunt me, especially at night when I'm in my bed. So I try to get to sleep quickly.

In the war, I remember shooting this one bloke. I thought, "Should I?" and I remember saying, "Sorry mate." But it was him or me. I have no regrets. I would do all the same things again. The only thing is, when you get to a certain age you don't need much sleep. If I get six hours I think I've overslept. I've been seeing Vi more often, especially if I doze after dinner and I wake up and hear her. I see her for a second and it's only the wireless that's woken me up and I feel just fine. I always said "good night" to her and tell her "I love her" from the day we got married. So, every night since she passed away, I go into her bedroom and still say it and tonight being bingo night before I go, I say "Good night" to her and ask her to make me shout "House!" But sometimes she never hears me so I say, "If I win I will come and wake you up". I still pay her numbers. But now she lets me keep what I've won. I still put flowers in her room.

Well, this afternoon I'm in the club at two o'clock for a party with my young friends and old comrades. The eldest is ninety. We never give up. It's to celebrate the end of WW2 in Europe, VE Day, and we will probably fight it again after a few JD's (Jack Daniels) this afternoon. We never gave up then, and we were only boys then.

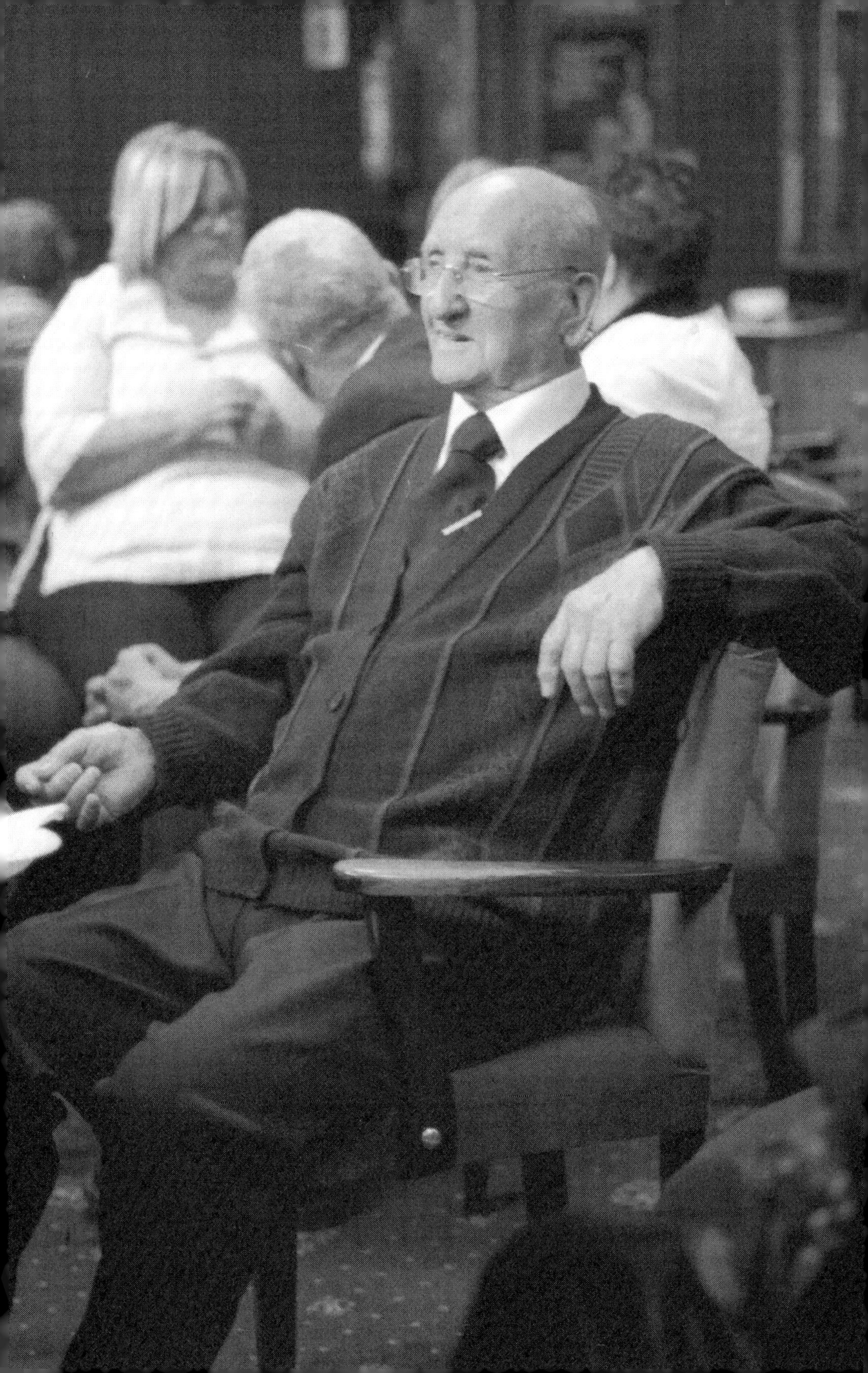

Chapter Eleven

A FORGOTTEN MAN REMEMBERED

Early in 2019, Jane Davies, the curator of the Lancashire Regiments at Fullwood barracks in Preston Lancashire, invited Raymond to visit the museum. I had contacted her and visited several weeks earlier to talk about the research I wanted to do to tell Ray's story. The museum were very keen to meet him. She and her colleagues thought that everyone from 1st South Lancs had died. Jane arranged for passes for Ray and some of his friends from the St Helens veterans' breakfast club. She said she would take us round the exhibits, show him some of the photographs, documents and war maps about the 1st South Lancs held in the museum's archives. Ray was delighted to receive the invite so we made the arrangements.

A group of us met in the car park outside the museum and, after clearing security, were admitted in. Raymond was shown round all the exhibits in the museum personally by Jane. On several occasions he fell silent and became emotional as though something he had seen had triggered a distant memory. He recognised old comrades in the grainy black-and-white photographs, all of these friends long gone. The rest of us kept a respectful distance and allowed him these moments alone with his thoughts and memories. He hadn't seen these faces for 75 years.

Jane kindly laid on sandwiches and tea and coffee for us all. Some of the other museum staff and even the Colonel himself came down to meet and talk to Raymond. We were served the refreshments on a long polished mahogany table that dominated the room. We were told that it had been "liberated" by the regiment from a German general's office somewhere in Germany, an action we said Ray would approve of and which made me think back to his story about the Bayeux tapestry.

A special treat for Ray was meeting a serving soldier from the regiment. They chatted together for short while. No doubt Ray was telling him how it was done "in his day". He was delighted to meet this soldier and I think he came away from the chat knowing that his old regiment was in very good and safe hands.

The museum kindly agreed to display Ray's paintings he had painted about some of his experiences in the war and some of the actions he had been in. Until his health made it difficult, he was a prolific artist. His depictions of some of the images buried in his mind are heart-breaking. We are eternally grateful to Jane for all her trouble. The visit made Raymond very happy.

In July 2018, Ray was honoured with an invite to attend the Armed Services Day at St. Helens rugby club, an annual event when the club celebrates all members of the armed forces past and present. Ray had been a supporter of the club all of his life. He was given a VIP invitation, and honoured with a lavish three-course pre-match dinner at the club's restaurant. Before kick-off, he made his way down from the best seat in the house to edge of the pitch. The players of both teams and veteran members of the armed forces formed a guard of honour. The crowd of 10,500 people gave him a standing ovation when he walked out.

Raymond Rush: I was given the match ball to take out. I had to walk through the guard of honour to the middle of the pitch and give the ball to the referee. I was so nervous I couldn't stop shaking. Thankfully I was steadied by two lovely ladies. One on each arm. Kerry Sutton, my cousin's wife, and Samantha Jane, who ran the veterans' breakfast club. I'd never been the centre of attention for anything up until then.

I had, that same year, been awarded the French *Chevaliers de la Légion d'honneur* medal for helping to free them from the Nazis, and I was presented with it at half-time by Eamonn McManus, the chairman of St. Helens Rugby Club. I'd asked him to present it to me, instead of a politician, because I had a lot of respect for what he had done for the people of St. Helens. Mr. McManus told me his father was a veteran of the Burma campaign in World War Two.

Jon Wilkin, the club Captain, ran up to me and shook my hand and said, "It was great to meet a true hero." He thanked me for my war service. It was lovely of him to do that. He didn't have to.

The ceremony was broadcast live on television. The commentators read out a tribute to Raymond that had been printed in the match day programme. People from all round the country wrote in to say how impressed they were with the Saints club to celebrate a national hero in the way that they did.

Kerry Sutton, Raymond Rush and Samantha Jane at St.Helens Rugby Club, July 2nd 2018 © Bernard Platt, St Helens Star.

2019 saw the 75th anniversary of the D-Day landings. No expense was spared by the Royal British Legion in organizing a cruise for their D-Day veterans across to the Normandy beaches. There were to be receptions and commemorations and Services of Remembrance. The veterans were to meet members of the Royal Family along with other world leaders. They would be wined and dined and given an opportunity to tell their stories to the world. This was a once in a lifetime opportunity for people of all ages to thank our veterans from the liberating armies for their selfless service, and to remember those young men who paid the ultimate price for freedom.

Raymond Rush: I was so excited to get the invitation from the Legion to attend. I've got some problems with my legs and had to go into hospital for a short time. I was okay but I had to get it sorted. I found out that the Legion had taken me off the trip because one of their people misunderstood my health and mobility and said it would be too much trouble to take me. To this day I can't understand why they did this.

As an alternative they said I should make my own way to London, get on their bus to Southampton and get a boat for Normandy, i.e. miss all the celebrations with The Queen. I was devastated and gave up on things. I couldn't take it any longer. Once I found out I was off the trip it finished me off. The trip was to give me closure but, because I couldn't go, it's all still with me. So telling my story in this book will get it all off my chest. I can wrap it up and put it to bed and forget about it all. I've been a Royal British Legion member for over sixty years and I've never asked them for anything. They should have done me some access ramps in my house like they promised.[1] They promised me a two-week holiday in Byng House in Southport and now they're closing it. They have never contacted me ever over all these years. One time at the breakfast club, a Liverpool British Legion representative was there and she said they would have my name inscribed on a slab in Hero's Walk. They never came back with anything. That was the last I heard about it. I've given up on the British Legion.

When Ray found out he had been taken off the Royal British Legion list for Normandy we, his friends and fellow veterans, organized a reception and party for him in the hospital to thank him for his service to our country on D-Day. With the blessing of the hospital management and staff, we dressed in berets and ties and got him a cake and a can of Guinness. The hospital management very kindly attended as did some of the nursing staff. Raymond proudly wore his beret with his adored South Lancs cap badge and displayed his medals proudly across his chest. Visitors to the hospital and other staff delighted him by asking for a photograph with him and listened to his stories. I had never seen him so happy.

---

1. Months later, the Legion did contact him and apologise, saying his application had "fallen through the cracks" and they would build the ramp. But by the time this offer came through, Raymond had made the decision to move into a care home.

Because he missed the trip we wrote on his behalf to Her Majesty the Queen explaining what had happened. She very kindly replied to him personally which also made him very happy. But on recovering from his illness and leaving hospital, the first thing Raymond Rush did was cancel his British Legion membership, to which he had paid thousands over the years.

Surprise for D-Day veteran Ray

By Kelsey Maxwell
news@sthelensstar.co.uk

A 95-YEAR-OLD D-Day veteran, who was disappointed to not be able to travel to Normandy for the 75th anniversary commemorations, was surprised by a special party in his honour at Whiston Hospital.

Raymond, who was born in Prescot in 1923, joined the 1st Battalion of the South Lancashire regiment in September 1942 and was part of the first wave landing on Sword Beach, Normandy on June 6, 1944.

He saw action in France, Holland and Belgium and finished up in Croatia.

He was demobbed in 1948 and returned to St Helens, where he set up as a pig farmer before going on to work at Greenalls brewery.

Raymond, who was awarded France's highest honour the Legion d'Honneur in June, was upset that he had to miss his official trip to Normandy with the Royal British Legion because he was in hospital with a leg infection.

However, his friends at St Helens Armed Forces and Veterans Breakfast Club surprised him on Thursday, June 6 by organising a special commemoration just for him at Whiston Hospital.

Speaking to the Star, a very surprised Raymond, who wore his military medals and beret with pride on the day, said: "I am absolutely made up. It is terrific.

"I don't know a lot of these people so it's nice that they have come here for me."

His cousin Pat Harrop, 70, from Newton-le-Willows, added: "It's wonderful to have this for Ray today, because he was just devastated when he found out he couldn't go to Normandy.

"He got an infection in his leg and wasn't safe to travel. It's been on the TV all day I bet he saw it and felt down, so it's good that he's had this instead.

"We are very proud of Ray. He was only 21 when he joined and did it because his brother Arthur went missing in action and was never found.

"His first day of action was D-Day so it's important to celebrate him on days like this."

A poignant moment during the celebration, which was attended by more than 30 people, was when a hospital staff member who was born on D-Day thanked Ray for his service.

Lucy McLoughlin, from Blackbrook, who worked as a voluntary chaplain at the hospital and celebrated her 75th birthday on Thursday, June 6, added: "I was born on D-Day 75 years ago, the day he fought.

"So when I heard what was happening with him today I was just amazed and had to thank him and all those who fought with him for what they did.

"When I think of the sacrifice of this man and others like him, I realise how lucky we all are to have them."

Raymond was recently awarded the Legion d'Honneur – an honour that France bestows on those who risked their lives to liberate their country from the Nazis during the Second World War.

He featured in the Star last year when he appeared on the pitch at half-time of a Saints match against Wakefield in June last year.

Many other people visiting the hospital came up to Ray to shake his hand, get a picture with him and thank him for his service. Ray added: "I feel a bit famous."

He was also visited by the chief executive of the hospital Ann Marr and chairman Richard Fraser.

Ray was shocked but surprised by the party

St. Helens Star

Catholic Church at Maashees destroyed during the battle in 1944.

The War Memorial in Smakt-Holthees.

Chapter Twelve

OVERLOON 75 YEARS ON

75 years later and Raymond Rush had never forgotten his friend, John Mather. As Ray got older, thoughts of family, home, work and the other things we all have in our lives receded and older memories started to take prominence. If we could locate where John Mathers grave was, we would take Raymond back to Holland so that he could see John one last time. In the meantime, contact with Janneke Kennis, the curator of the excellent museum in Overloon dedicated to the Second War World, had resulted in yet another friendship between a 1st South Lancs man and an inhabitant of Overloon.

Just before Armistice Day 2019, a package from Janneke arrived for Ray. From the museum, she had very kindly sent a book about the battle of Overloon and Venray and a dvd of old footage taken during operations by 1st South Lancs during that terrible winter of 1944. Ray invited us round to his care home to drink a Guinness with him and watch the DVD. We watched silently while he saw sights that he hadn't seen for 75 years. He could remember towns and villages. He could recall the woods. The devastation of the once beautiful towns shown on the screen took him right back. But most of all it reminded him of the friendship between the South Lancs and the people of these towns. I think if you were to ask him was it worth the sacrifice made by so many worth it and he would reply, "Yes."

Sometime in late November 2019, Ray's cousin, Ian Sutton, found out where in Holland John Mather was buried. He was buried in a War Graves cemetery on the edge of a small village called Mook, just to the north of Overloon. The grave was lovingly tended by the local children. We started to organize a trip for Raymond to Overloon and Venray. We would take him to see his friend this last time even if we had to carry him. There is an. The staff came on board as soon as they were told about Raymond. Here was one of the few men left who drove out the Nazis and gave the grateful people of these towns their lives back. Of course they would treat him like the hero he is.

Flights and hotels were booked. A visit to the museum and a grand lunch were organized by our new friends in Overloon. The mayor of the principality would be joining us and Raymond would get the chance to wear his medals and his old beret proudly displaying the cap badge of the South Lancs.

January 2020 saw a flu-like virus emerge from China. It quickly threatened to overrun not only Asia but the whole world. It spread and soon was in Europe. Once it was in Holland and the UK there was nothing else for it. Raymond's trip would have to be cancelled until the virus had been defeated. He settled into his care home and prepared to wait it out.

He was diagnosed with Covid-19 on V. E. Day 10th, May 2020. The doctor refused to attend the care home due to the infection and issued a do-not-resuscitate order (DNR). Ambulance crews twice refused to take Ray to hospital and re-issued the DNR. Although the care home were doing everything they could for Ray, they could not provide oxygen or the further medical treatment that Ray required. After increasing pressure from his cousin, Ian, and the care home, he was eventually taken to hospital.

The grave of John Mather at Mook War Cemetery,
at Limburg, near Nijmegen.

Old soldier remembers
by Raymond Rush, 2011

They're marching past the cenotaph
They're standing tall and straight
They're laying wreaths and poppies
And they're preaching love and hate
Tell them padre, tell them
As war is not worth the toss
There never ain't no victories
Just an awful loss.
It's more than 60 years ago
Since I went to fight old Fritz
He needed teaching well, we'd stitch him up real tight
It would only take a month or two
We'd show him what was what
Then all come home as heroes
Wearing medals like as not.
Those stretched into years and years
Tell them padre tell how marching to adventure
Became a crawl to hell.
One day perhaps its yesterday, its same you see
We came upon the enemy
As near to you as me
I opened fire I had no choice.
But firing I could see
Inside the German uniform
Were just a boy like me.
And when my bullets hit him
I could hear, it weren't that far
How in his dying agony
He screamed out for his Ma.
And therefore and then I knew the truth
As clear as clear could be
How I'd just killed my brother
I were him and he were me.
No, I don't need no poppies
My memories never cease
They're graven on my very soul
For me there is no peace.

Raymond remembers a poems that has been with him and his thoughts for many years. The author is unknown to us but it has great meaning for Ray and has comforted him during some difficult times.

> It's only a piece of Khaki
> Treasured along with pride
> Part of your Daddies tunic
> Who like a hero died
> Fighting for love and freedom
> Mother and little one.
> It's only a piece of Khaki
> That your daddy wore at Mons.
> It's only a piece of Khaki
> Treasured along with pride
> Part of your daddy's tunic
> Who like a hero died.
> Now the fighting was all finished
> Was the closing of the day
> The British were outnumbered
> Ten to one the papers say.
> He saw his Captain wounded
> So he hastened to his side
> For better love had no one
> That's how your daddy died.
> Just a piece of Khaki
> Treasured along with pride.

Raymond Rush: I first heard that monologue in our Club at the 90th anniversary of the RBL. I had never seen so many men just let their emotions flow, not a dry eye. It was said with such passion. As you get older you get more emotional. It just seems to take over at the least thing. A look or a word in the wrong way and it sets you thinking, you go back in time and start remembering things you want to forget.

I often wonder what people think of me. My teacher called me a ruffian. Well I think I was then, but I know the people who I worked with and my old comrades showed me some respect, like the young chap carrying his baby, who came to my side marching to the Cenotaph. He grabbed my hand and shook it. All he said was "Thank You". I thought, well that's respect. I never saw him again, probably he had a veteran Grandad. They never called us heroes like they do now. When you was in uniform during the war people could not do enough for you, but when you were demobbed you were forgotten.

Raymond Rush
St. Helens, December 2019

RAYMOND RUSH
1923-2020

1st South Lancashire Regiment

Raymond Rush died at Whiston Hospital, St. Helens
on 23 May 2020

Appendix 1

From: Ian Sutton
Sent: Sunday, October 20, 2019 11:41 PM
To: Gillian McKinnon
Subject: D Day Veteran Ray Rush

Dear Gillian,

I have written this email numerous times and have now decided to draft it in a facts format as we see it. Firstly let me introduce ourselves. I am Ian Sutton and I am a relative of Ray's. I am an ex-Army warrant officer with 27-years regular service. Ray is a D-Day veteran with the South Lancashire Regiment. He was the first to land on the first wave on Sword beach in 1944. Out of all those in his landing craft, he was the only one to make it to Germany unharmed. He fought in every major battle in WW2. In addition, he has been a fully paid up member of the British Legion for over 40+ years.

The events, as we saw them are as follows:

1. Ray was one of the first 200 veterans to apply for the cruise to Portsmouth and Normandy.

2. Ray received confirmation of his place for the cruise along with a pack detailing the breakdown of events. In addition he was sent photographs of his cabin and the ship. To say he was excited was an understatement.

3. Ray had caught an infection which put him in hospital but that was not going to prevent him going. He was making good progress and was walking with the aid of a stick and telling all those that treated him of his pending cruise to Normandy.

4. With no explanation he was then informed that he was to make his own way to London where he will be driven to Portsmouth where a ferry would take him to Caen. He would be accommodated at a hotel but he was not going on the cruise. No reasons were given.

5. This was very upsetting to Ray and as consequence he gave up, he became bedridden and very ill.

6. We were informed that the British Legion would now fund three of us to travel to London and that I was to book flights/trains and that I would be reimbursed.

7. Ray was making a slow recovery and not keen in anything else other than the cruise. Had I booked the flights and Ray not travel I wasn't sure if I would get my money back. We then decided that he wouldn't go.

8. Just over 250 veterans travelled on the cruise that was booked for 300.

We feel that Ray has been let down by the very club he has supported for 40 years plus. He looked at the cruise as a chance to 'let it all out' with fellow veterans and finally put his demons behind him and he had hopes of meeting Royalty taken away. To be given a place and have that taken away, without explanation, was totally wrong and nearly killed him.

What we are asking is for the person who made this call and their reasons for doing so? I feel the minimum he deserves is an explanation.

Raymond is very unique in that he is the only living person from the South Lancashire Regiment left alive, the last man standing. He was the 1st man at 7.30am to face machine guns on Sword beech and the last one to come home.

He is a national hero but no one appears interested in his story other than his close circle of friends. We feel with time against us that should change.

I hope you can help us on this matter
Kind regards

Ian Sutton and Ray Rush

Patron Her Majesty The Queen

The Royal British Legion
25-31 Williamson Street
Liverpool
L1 1EB

T   0333 011 4100
E   gmckinnon@britishlegion.org.uk
W   britishlegion.org.uk

Legion Contact Centre
0808 802 8080

Registered Charity Number: 219279

Mr Ian Sutton
428 Chisley Lane
Haydock
St. Helens

6th November 2019

Dear Mr Sutton

Thank you for contacting us on behalf of Mr Rush who unfortunately was unable to attend the D-Day commemorative events in Normandy. Sincere apologies for taking so long to respond, as you can appreciate we are very busy building up to and during the Poppy Appeal.

As you can no doubt understand, organising these trips was very challenging for everyone involved and it was vitally important to ensure that whoever attended – either the boat or the other options of Caen and the NMA, received the best possible experience. We are eternally grateful for the sacrifice given by all the veterans in Normandy and recognised the need to say thank you to those remaining veterans for their huge contribution and these options were designed to ensure a non-discriminatory approach to a generation of veterans who could potentially be experiencing a number of health and mobility problems. With this in mind, we tried to ensure each experience was accessible. Furthermore, we absolutely needed to ensure we addressed a variety of other legislative and legal processes like GDPR, Health & Safety and maritime law (for Boudicca). We therefore embarked on an additional exercise of obtaining more in-depth health and mobility information as veterans would need to embark on a long and difficult journey, to get to each of these options and we needed to make sure that we were not putting anyone at risk when they undertook this journey.

Denise met with you both at the breakfast club on 4th April 2019 and asked you the same question all the D-Day veterans who had registered, had been asked. The report received from Denise stated:

"I met both Ray and his cousin Ian at St Helens breakfast club on 4th April. Although Ray is very independent, lives alone and cares for himself both personal and medical, he would find climbing the steps of a coach very difficult, Ian his cousin suggested some coach companies provide steps to make the steps less deep. The size of the cabin and bathroom/toilet would be OK for both Ray and Ian however Ray would not be able to step in/out of a bath so a walk in shower would be necessary.

Ray would also be taking his foldable electric wheelchair on the trip because although he can walk with only the use of one stick he cannot walk for long distances.

*Ray has arthritis in his hands, knees and he also has gout. Several medications are taken one each day (Furosemide, Finasteride, Bisoprolol, Bicalutamide, Allopurinol, Simvastatin, Ramipril, Warfarin) which he administers himself, he does not use any needles/sharps. The only medical condition Ian has is an allergy to dust and they are OK to share a room. Both passports are well in date (Ray 27/8/23 & Ian 13/12/20) as are EHIC cards (Ray 28/3/24 & Ian 28/3/24). Ian has no mobility issues at all and they would both be willing to take part in PR. **Ray does not mind the boat or hotel** he just really wants to go to Normandy and meet other veterans. They both have a credit or debit card and no medical/mobility equipment requires batteries apart from the foldable wheelchair."*

Registered Charity: The Royal British Legion, Haig House, 199 Borough High Street, London SE1 1AA

-2-

This was then evaluated by the Assistant Director for North, Mrs Nicola Cook alongside the representatives from the Coach Company and Boudicca, and given that Mr Rush clearly stated that **"he did not mind the boat or the Hotel he just wants to go to Normandy"**....it was decided that Caen would be the better option for and this was subsequently communicated to him.

On 23rd May we received an email sent by Mr Burns on your behalf, complaining about the cost to get to London, which I responded to immediately stating *"I am more than happy to cover any travel costs in order to get Mr Rush and his carer to London and I have instructed a member of my team to contact Mr Rush and make these arrangements with him. We are keen for Mr Rush to have an enjoyable experience and will help in whatever way we can"*. Denise then made contact and I believe that Mr Rush was sadly admitted to hospital in June some time – near the date of the trip. I am not sure when this was exactly but I recall being told that Mr Rush was not going to go on the trip due to his ill health. I realise that he was very disappointed to learn of the change from the voyage to the Hotel in Caen.

Mr Rush would have been accommodated by us in any way possible to get to Caen, which would have put him in the midst of his fellow D-Day veterans (which is what he wanted). We were already making all the relevant arrangements to get him there when we were advised he was not well.

The boat option was withdrawn when it was made very clear that he would struggle with steps – not only on the coach but on the boat as well. There were also very limited cabins with walk-in showers. With all this in mind it was decided that getting Mr Rush to Normandy was the primary focus so we moved him on to the Caen option. Mrs Nicola Cook, Assistant Director North, is willing to talk this through with you if you feel that may help with further clarity. If you would like me to pass your number on to her, please let me know. If you would like to contact Mrs Cook, her number is 07458 085494.

I know you are very disappointed that Mr Rush did not get on to Boudicca, but we really did follow due process and the alternative option would have got him to Normandy in a far safer way. I am sorry Mr Rush was not well enough to go to Caen in the end.

Please accept my sincere apologies if we fell short of our usual high standards.

Please pass on our fond regards to Mr Rush and our thanks for his contribution to the D-Day landings – we are eternally grateful.

Yours sincerely

Gillian McKinnon
Area Manager Cheshire & Merseyside

cc. Nicola Cook and Bob Gamble

Appendix 2

Ambassade de France
Londres

L'AMBASSADEUR

No 2018 - 1085712

18 April 2018

Dear Mr. Rush,

I have the pleasure of informing you that the President of the Republic has appointed you to the rank of *Chevalier* in the *Ordre national de la Légion d'honneur* by decree of 3 April 2018.

I offer you my warmest congratulations on this high honour, which recognizes your military engagement and steadfast involvement in the Liberation of France during the Second World War.

As we contemplate this Europe of peace, we must never forget the heroes like you who came from Britain and the Commonwealth to begin the liberation of Europe by liberating France. We owe our freedom and security to your dedication, because you were ready to risk your life.

I am happy to enclose your insignia and once again extend to you my heartfelt congratulations.

Yours sincerely,

Jean-Pierre Jouyet

Mr Raymond Vincent Rush
7 The Meadows
Rainhill, Prescot L35 0PQ

REFERENCES AND ACKNOWLEDGEMENTS

My thanks must go to the following people, sources and publications:

The South Lancs Regiment by Colonel B.R. Mullaly and *The First Battalion in the D-Day landings and the Normandy Battles, WW II* by The Lancashire Infantry Museum.

Events of the battles for La Londe are taken from contributor threads on www.w2talk.com – Captain Edwards 246 Field Company RE and Corporal G. Penter, B Company 1st Battalion South Lancs.

www.tracesofwar.com / www.argunners.com
facebook - prescot online / www.britannica.com
www.atlanticwall.com / www.lightbobs.com
www.w2talk.com / www.holland.com
www.roll-of-honour.com

The South Lancs Regiment PWV 1841–1958, Lancashire Regimental museum

The 1st battalion the South Lancs Regiment, Lancashire Regimental museum

Discussion threads and contributions taken from www.w2talk.com: "Château de la Londe".

C.P. Lamb, Grenadier Guards for his quote on the battle for Overloon.

Wim Baljet, who served with the Royal Army Ordnance Corps with the 3rd Infantry Division for his quote on 'Operation Aintree'.

Captain Edward K Deeming for his photograph.

The Robert Pearson Collection.

The staff and curator of The Duke of Lancaster's Regiment Lancashire Infantry

Eamonn McManus, Jon Wilkin, and all the staff, players and supporters at St. Helens Rugby League Club.

Bernard Platt and the staff at St Helens Star newspaper.

Janneke Kennis and the staff at Overloom War Museum.

Jane Davies, curator of the Lancashire Regiments at Fullwood barracks.

And finally thanks to Raymond for trusting me to tell his story.

Raymond Rush in 2015 standing on Sword Beach by the only current monument to the 1st South Lancashire Regiment. Photograph by Kerry Sutton.

Raymond Rush
The Last Man Standing

© John Kelly, Ian Sutton, 2020

June 6th 2020

ISBN: 9798648397224

John Kelly is identified as the author of this book.
The moral rights of the author have been asserted.

Published by Camera Journal, Cambridge

contact: camerajournal@hotmail.com

Book design by Paul Sutton

All rights reserved. No part of this publication may be reproduced or transmitted in any form or by any means electronic, mechanical, photocopying, recording, print on demand or otherwise, without the prior written permission of Camera Journal or the author.

Front cover: Raymond Rush in Italy.
D-Day painting by Raymond Rush.
Photograph on page 151 by Paul Sutton
Back cover: photograph by Bernard Platt.

Printed in Great Britain
by Amazon